New Testament
Storybook
for Kids

Illustrations by Lon Eric Craven

D1526654

CONCORDIA PUBLISHING HOUSE · SAINT LOUIS

Copyright © 2020 Concordia Publishing House
3558 S. Jefferson Ave., St. Louis, MO 63118-3968
1-800-325-3040 • cph.org

Text © 2018 Concordia Publishing House

Illustrations by Lon Eric Craven © 2018 Concordia Publishing House

Manufactured in East Peoria, IL/063692/340765

Table of Contents

The angel Gabriel tells the priest Zechariah he will have a baby who will prepare people for Jesus.

The Birth of John the Baptist Foretold

Have you ever prayed and asked God to do something for you but then given up when nothing happened?

When it was almost the time God wanted to send His Son into the world, He sent an angel named Gabriel (GAY-bree-uhl) to the temple in Jerusalem. Gabriel appeared to a priest who was burning incense in the Holy Place, the front room of the temple. The priest's name was Zechariah (zek-uh-RYE-uh). Zechariah and his wife, Elizabeth, both loved God and trusted His promise to send the Savior. Many years before, Zechariah had prayed that God would give them a child, but now they were very old, and no child had ever come.

When Gabriel suddenly appeared, Zechariah was terrified. The angel told him, "Do not be afraid, Zechariah, for your prayer has been heard, and your wife Elizabeth will bear you a son, and you shall call his name John."

The angel told him that his son would be great, and he would go before the Lord as His mighty messenger. He would prepare God's people to receive His Son, whom He had promised so long ago to Adam and Eve in the Garden of Eden after they had eaten the forbidden fruit.

This great promise surprised Zechariah very much. He answered, "How shall I know this? For I am an old man, and my wife is advanced in years." He didn't believe God's promise because he thought Elizabeth was way too old to have a baby.

The angel answered, "I am Gabriel. I stand in the presence of God, and I was sent to speak to you and to bring you this good news. And behold, you will be silent and unable to speak until the day that these things take place, because you did not believe my words, which will be fulfilled in their time." Sure enough, when the angel left him, Zechariah came out of the temple but couldn't say a word.

When his time to serve at the temple ended, he returned home and Elizabeth became pregnant, and the baby started growing inside her.

Sometimes, we pray for things, as Zechariah did, and it seems like God doesn't hear—or He doesn't care. But God hears all our prayers, and He promises to answer all of them. Sometimes, He gives us the things we ask for because those are best for us. Sometimes, He says no because He wants to give us something better than we could ever think of. Sometimes, He wants us to wait—like Zechariah—because His time has not come yet. But whatever His answer might be, you can be sure it will be the very best for you.

LET'S PRAY: Lord God, sometimes it is hard to keep praying—especially when we pray so hard and nothing seems to happen. Give me faith to trust in You and to believe Your promise to answer all my prayers. In Jesus' name. Amen.

The angel Gabriel tells Mary God has picked her to be the mother of His Son, Jesus.

Gabriel Visits Mary

When you look at a manger scene at Christmastime, what do you think about little baby Jesus?

Six months after Zechariah's wife, Elizabeth, became pregnant, God sent the angel Gabriel to a northern town called Nazareth to a young woman named Mary. She was betrothed to a man named Joseph. They had promised to marry each other and were waiting for their wedding, when they could move in together and start their family.

The angel appeared to Mary and said, "Greetings, O favored one, the Lord is with you!" Mary wasn't expecting an angel to come to her, and she was shaken up. She thought carefully about what he had said, and she wondered what he meant. She wondered what he was going to say to her next— would it be bad news or good news?

Gabriel said, "Do not be afraid, Mary, for you have found favor with God. And behold, you will bear a son, and you shall call His name Jesus." He told her this child would be great and would be called "the Son of the Most High."

Mary believed the angel, but she wondered how she would become the mother of this child. She wasn't married to Joseph yet.

The angel told her the Holy Spirit would come to her and use His mighty power to give her this baby. He added, "Therefore the child to be born will be called holy—the Son of God."

The angel said Jesus would be great; He would rule on the throne of His father David and reign over the house of Jacob forever. Mary knew this was the Savior God promised so long ago to Adam and Eve; to Abraham, Isaac, and Jacob; and to King David. Since He is God's own Son, His kingdom will never end.

Finally, the angel Gabriel told Mary that her relative Elizabeth was pregnant because of God's great power, even though she was way too old to have a baby.

Mary believed the angel. She was ready to offer herself to be part of God's loving plan. She replied, "I am the servant of the Lord; let it be to me according to your word."

It's neat that Jesus had a human mother just like you and me and every other boy and girl. Since Jesus lived as a boy on this earth, He knows what it is like to be a child, then grow up to be an adult, as you will one day. And since Jesus is a human, He was able to take our sins from us, carry them to the cross, and suffer and die there in our place.

But it's even better that Jesus' Father was God Almighty, and not a human birth father like our dads. That means Jesus doesn't have our sinful nature—He is holy and perfect. That means Jesus was able to keep all God's Commandments in our place and earn our place in heaven. And since He is God, Jesus was able to destroy the devil, death, and hell for us.

LET'S PRAY: Lord God, heavenly Father, thank You for the wonderful words the angel Gabriel brought to Mary. Thank You for sending Your only Son to be her Son, our strong Brother who saved us from our sins. In Jesus' name. Amen.

Mary visits Zechariah and his wife, Elizabeth. Their baby leaps because he is close to God's Son.

Mary Visits Elizabeth

Luke 1:39–56

Do you ever wish you could trade places with boys or girls who are more popular or have families with lots of money and things?

The angel Gabriel told Mary that God had chosen her to be the mother of His own Son. He also told her how God had used His great power to give a baby to her elderly relative Elizabeth. After the angel left, Mary decided to leave Nazareth and go visit Zechariah and Elizabeth in Judah (JOO-duh).

She traveled quickly and came to Zechariah's house. When she saw Elizabeth, Mary said hello. Right at that moment, Elizabeth's baby started leaping inside her. She was filled with the Holy Spirit and told Mary, "Blessed are you among women, and blessed is the fruit of your womb! And why is this granted to me that the mother of my Lord should come to me?" Yes, even though Mary hadn't said a word about being pregnant, Elizabeth knew she was carrying a baby, and she knew this baby was the Lord, the promised Son of God.

Mary was amazed God had chosen her to be the mother of His precious Son. Mary was not famous; her family wasn't powerful; they didn't have a lot of money. Yet God chose her. He passed by all the rich, powerful, and famous families, and chose Mary of Nazareth to be the mother of His Son. She began praising Him in words we call "The Song of Mary": "My soul magnifies the Lord, and my spirit rejoices in God my Savior." The more Mary thought about it, the more she realized how amazing God is. "He who is mighty has done great things for me, and holy is His name." And she praised God for keeping His promise to Abraham, Isaac, and Jacob: "He has helped His servant Israel, in remembrance of His mercy, as He spoke to our fathers, to Abraham and to his offspring forever."

Mary spent three months with Zechariah and Elizabeth. These must have been wonderful days, talking about God's great love and feeling the babies grow inside them.

God didn't choose Mary and Elizabeth because they had a lot of friends or nice big homes or a bunch of money. He chose them because He loved them. God chose you for the same reason. It doesn't matter to Him if everyone at school knows you or not or likes you or not. It doesn't matter if your family has a lot of money or none at all. God gave His own Son, Jesus, to save you, and He made you His own child in Baptism. Now, He wants to work through you to make other boys and girls His own sons and daughters through faith in Jesus.

LET'S PRAY: Lord God, heavenly Father, thank You for choosing me to be Your child and for saving me through Your Son, Jesus. Give me Your Holy Spirit, that I may be brave and filled with love and joy to tell other people about Jesus' great love. In Jesus' name. Amen.

After Mary returns home, Elizabeth gives birth to a son, and Zechariah names him John.

The Birth of John the Baptist Luke 1:57–80

Did you ever have to keep a secret from someone and it was almost impossible to do so?

Mary stayed with Zechariah and Elizabeth until the time came for John the Baptist to be born. Then Mary returned home to Nazareth. When Elizabeth had her baby, all their neighbors celebrated with them and praised God for being so good and kind to them.

All this time, Zechariah remained silent, unable to speak—but surely he watched and listened and had so much he wanted to say! All through the nearly three months Mary had stayed with them, he couldn't say a word. And even after his baby was born, he still couldn't talk.

One more week went by, and Zechariah's son turned eight days old. For Israelite boys, this eighth day was very special. This was the day they were circumcised and given their very own names. Zechariah and Elizabeth's neighbors and relatives gathered to celebrate.

When it was time to name the baby, the guests wanted to name him Zechariah, after his father. But Elizabeth said, "No; he shall be called John." The neighbors and relatives were puzzled: "None of your relatives is called by this name." They turned to Zechariah to see what he wanted to name him. Zechariah took a writing tablet and wrote down in front of them all, "His name is John."

Suddenly, God opened Zechariah's mouth so he could talk again. Now at last, after holding all his thoughts inside for almost a year, Zechariah was able to praise and thank God the way he should have done when the angel Gabriel first spoke to him.

Zechariah was filled with the Holy Spirit and said some wonderful words we call the "Song of Zechariah." We call it a song because sometimes we sing it in church. In his song, he praised God for sending His Son to be our Savior, and he rejoiced that the promised Savior had come. He didn't say it in his song, but he knew that wonderful baby had been right there in his house, growing inside the Virgin Mary.

Then Zechariah looked at his own little baby. He told John, "And you, child, will be called the prophet of the Most High; for you will go before the Lord to prepare His ways." When John grew up, he did go before the Christ and made people ready to hear their Savior's wonderful words. Zechariah closed his song by speaking again about Mary's baby and the wonderful peace and eternal life He would win for all of us.

Keeping secrets is hard—especially when we have great good news to tell people. But the greatest, most happy news of all is something we never have to keep secret from our family, friends, and people at school and everywhere: God loves them and sent His Son to save them.

LET'S PRAY: Lord God, heavenly Father, thank You for bringing Zechariah to bold faith and confidence in Your promises, and for restoring his voice to tell all his relatives and neighbors that Your Son was coming at last. Give me confidence to tell everyone I know about how You sent Your Son as our Savior, so they, too, may know all about Jesus. In Jesus' name. Amen.

In a dream, an angel tells Joseph not to be afraid to take Mary as his wife because her baby is God's Son.

An Angel Visits Joseph

Do you know children who live without their father or mother? What do you think is the worst part of that?

The time came for God to keep His promise to send the Savior. By the power of the Holy Spirit, His Son became a human baby, growing inside His mother, the Virgin Mary. When Joseph learned she was going to have a baby, that made him sad. He wanted Mary to be his wife and live with him in their home. He wanted to have babies together and raise their own family.

Joseph loved Mary very much and was worried about what would happen to her if he left her and made her raise her baby by herself. But for Joseph, it was even more important to do what God wanted. One of God's Ten Commandments says, "You shall not commit adultery." That means God wants babies to come from a mother and a father who are already married to each other.

As Joseph thought and prayed about it, he was afraid God would be upset with him if he married her. So Joseph decided to divorce Mary. But he would do it quietly, not telling anyone why he was ending their marriage. That would protect Mary from people who might want to hurt her.

After he made up his mind, Joseph fell asleep. But in his dreams, an angel told him not to be afraid to take Mary as his wife. The baby growing inside her was God's Son. The Lord wanted Joseph to give Mary's baby the name *Jesus* and raise Him as if He were his own son. The name *Jesus* means "the Lord saves." It was the perfect name for this baby, because He was the promised Savior, the Son of God, who saved us from our sins.

Joseph woke up from his dream and did everything the Lord told him to do. He took Mary as his wife. So when baby Jesus was born, Joseph was there to take care of Him like a father.

God loves you very much too, just like He loved His own Son, Jesus, and Joseph and Mary. If your mom and dad are living together with you, thank God for keeping them together. If they aren't together anymore and you are growing up with one but not the other, or if you aren't living with either your mother or your father, that is hard.

But remember that God will never forget you. He loves you and will always be by your side. He will give you everything you need and will wash away all your sins for Jesus' sake. And one more thing: Even if you don't have your mother or father with you anymore, God has made you His very own son or daughter for Jesus' sake. He is your heavenly Father, who will never grow old, get sick, or die. He'll never get tired of taking care of you and leave. He is in heaven right now preparing your forever home.

LET'S PRAY: Lord God, heavenly Father, thank You for making sure Joseph was there to be a father to Jesus, even though he wasn't Jesus' birth father. Thank You for choosing me as Your own child for Jesus' sake when You baptized me. Help me to serve You well and show the world what a great God and Savior I have. In Jesus' name. Amen.

In the little town of Bethlehem, Mary gives birth to baby Jesus and lays Him in a manger.

The Birth of Jesus

What are some things you do to celebrate Jesus' birth at Christmas?

The time was coming for Mary to have her baby. Since this was God's own Son, you might expect Him to have been born in a big, shiny palace near the temple in the big city of Jerusalem. But God had very different plans.

Joseph and Mary were living and working in Nazareth, far to the north, when suddenly a command came from the emperor of Rome, Caesar Augustus. Luke wrote, "In those days a decree went out from Caesar Augustus that all the world should be registered. . . . And all went to be registered, each to his own town" (Luke 2:1, 3).

Caesar wanted to count how many people were in his empire. So Joseph had to go to his family's home town. It wasn't Jerusalem; it was the little town of Bethlehem (BETH-leh-hem), the home of his ancestor David.

But that was exactly what God had said would happen. Through the prophet Micah, God promised, "But you, O Bethlehem Ephrathah, who are too little to be among the clans of Judah, from you shall come forth for Me one who is to be ruler in Israel, whose coming forth is from of old, from ancient days" (Micah 5:2). God used a command from the Roman emperor to make the prophecy of Micah come true. Before the world was created, the Son of God came forth from His Father. And here in the little town of Bethlehem, He would be born to be ruler in Israel.

So Joseph and Mary left Nazareth and made their way to Bethlehem. By the time they arrived, the little town was full of Jewish descendants of David who had come to town to be counted. Joseph looked around for a place where he and Mary could stay, but it was a small town and he couldn't find any good place for Mary to have her baby. Every guest room was full.

Since he couldn't find a place inside a house or building, Joseph was forced to take Mary into a cave or stable where work animals like donkeys and oxen were kept out of the wind and rain. He cleared a little spot between the animals and made a bed for Mary. That's where Mary had her baby, God's own Son. She wrapped Him tightly in swaddling cloths, and since she didn't have a crib, she laid Him in a manger, the trough that held the animals' food.

That is hardly where we would expect to find God's newly born Son. He is so great and wonderful, He should have been lying in a soft, beautiful crib in a huge, warm palace. But the Son of God lay in straw, surrounded by the animals He created. He didn't come to be served by people but to serve them. God kept His promises to Adam and Eve; Abraham, Isaac, and Jacob; and King David. Their Descendant—the promised Savior—was born. He was finally here.

LET'S PRAY: Lord God, thank You for keeping Your promise to send Your Son to save us. Each Christmas, help me remember that His coming is the reason Christmas is so special. In Jesus' name. Amen.

An angel tells nearby shepherds the good news
that the Savior has been born in Bethlehem.

The Angels and the Shepherds

What is your favorite present that you ever got for Christmas?

When Jesus was born, Mary wrapped Him in strips of cloth and laid Him in a manger, a feeding trough for animals.

In the fields outside of Bethlehem, shepherds were watching their sheep in the night. Suddenly, an angel appeared to them. He was shining in glory, and the even brighter glory of God was shining around them. This filled the shepherds with fear. The bright light and the shining angel reminded them of their sins and how they deserved to be punished by God.

But the angel told them, "Fear not, for behold, I bring you good news of great joy that will be for all the people. For unto you is born this day in the city of David a Savior, who is Christ the Lord." This was the promise God had given to Adam and Eve in the Garden of Eden and to so many others throughout the Old Testament.

What an amazing moment for the shepherds! The long-promised Savior had finally come—and He was somewhere over there in the little town of Bethlehem. The angel told them, "You will find a baby wrapped in swaddling cloths and lying in a manger." When they went searching through the town, they would be sure they had found the right baby.

When the angel finished, suddenly the sky was filled with angels who praised God and said, "Glory be to God on high, and on the earth, peace among those with whom He is pleased." God is pleased with us when we turn from our sins and trust His promise to forgive us for Jesus' sake. When our sins are forgiven, we have peace with God.

When the angels returned to heaven, the shepherds left their sheep and rushed off at once into Bethlehem to find the baby. When they found Him, they told Mary and Joseph what the angel had said to them. Mary listened closely and thought about what God was teaching her about her Son, our amazing Savior.

Then the shepherds went back to the fields. But they didn't keep the great news to themselves. The angel had said his good news was for *all* the people—and it would bring great joy to all who heard and believed God's promise to save them. The shepherds told people about the wonderful things God had done, and they praised Him for keeping His promise and sending His Son.

There are many things about Christmas that are really exciting. Certainly, the presents are part of that. You may get something so great you can't wait to tell your friends all about it. That is how the shepherds felt about the good news they had heard. The Savior of all people was born, and they had seen Him with their own eyes! They couldn't keep the good news to themselves. That same excitement makes it hard to keep the joy of Jesus' birth to ourselves.

LET'S PRAY: Heavenly Father, You sent an angel to tell the shepherds the good news of Jesus' birth. Like the shepherds, help me understand how great Jesus really is so that I trust Him as my Savior and am excited to tell the Good News to everyone I meet. In Jesus' name. Amen.

When Joseph and Mary bring Jesus to the temple,
two older believers see the promised Savior.

The Presentation of Jesus

What do you think it would have been like to hold baby Jesus and know you were holding God's Son?

When Jesus was forty days old, Joseph and Mary took Him to Jerusalem. Moses' Law required each firstborn boy to be presented to the Lord at the temple when he was forty days old. That very day, Joseph and Mary brought God's own Son to the temple to be presented to God His Father.

While they were there, Mary and Joseph met two older Jews. The first was a man named Simeon. Simeon loved God and was waiting for Him to send the Messiah. The Holy Spirit had revealed to him that he would see the Christ before he died. At this very time, the Holy Spirit led him to the temple and revealed to him that this baby Jesus was that promised Savior. Simeon took Jesus in his arms and said, "Lord, now You are letting Your servant go in peace, because my own eyes have seen Your salvation, which You have prepared before the face of all people."

We call this the "Song of Simeon." Sometimes, we sing it in church after we receive Holy Communion. We can go from the altar at peace and forgiven by God because our eyes have seen the body and blood of our Lord and Savior in the bread and wine. We remember Jesus died on the cross to save us from our sin.

When Simeon finished these words, he turned to Mary and told her that not everyone was going to be happy that Jesus was born. Some would reject Him and refuse to believe in Him. And Mary would feel great sorrow, like a sword piercing through her soul. Simeon was talking about the day when Mary would stand under Jesus' cross and watch Him die for her sins and ours.

There at the temple along with Simeon was an old, old woman named Anna. Her husband had died long ago when she was still a young woman. Now, she never left the temple but worshiped God and prayed night and day. After she saw Jesus, she spoke about Him to everyone who was waiting for the Messiah.

Simeon and Anna spent their whole lives believing in God and waiting for Him to keep His promise to send His Son. God has promised to send Jesus on Judgment Day to repair His broken creation, to raise the dead, and to give eternal life with Him to you and all believers. Just like Simeon and Anna, you can watch for Jesus' return when you worship God in church, when you read and study your Bible at home and in Sunday School and Bible class, and when you get older, each time you receive Jesus' body and blood in Holy Communion. The Holy Spirit will keep you ready until the day when you can see Jesus' face, just like Simeon and Anna did.

LET'S PRAY: Lord God, thank You for these two older believers who got to see and hold Jesus. Give me such faith and joy all through my life that I may always praise Jesus and tell others what He has done to save us, then be ready to see Him with my own eyes in heaven. In Jesus' name. Amen.

Wise Men follow the star from far away. They give
Jesus gold, frankincense, and myrrh.

The Visit of the Wise Men

Have you ever been afraid a new boy or girl would come and take your friends away?

When Jesus was born, God His Father put a special star up in the sky. Far away in the East, a group of Wise Men saw it. They gathered gifts together and started following its light. The star led them to the land of Israel. When they reached the big city of Jerusalem, they visited King Herod (HAIR-uhd) and asked where they could find the baby who was born the King of the Jews.

Some people called him Herod the Great because he spent many years improving the temple that the exiles rebuilt when they returned from Babylon. It was beautiful and magnificent. But Herod was a very nervous king. He didn't want anyone to take his kingdom away from him. When the Wise Men said the King of the Jews had been born, he got really scared.

King Herod knew the Jewish people were expecting a Savior. So he asked the priests where the Christ Child was to be born. They read to him the words of the prophet Micah, "And you, O Bethlehem, in the land of Judah, are by no means least among the rulers of Judah; for from you shall come a ruler who will shepherd My people Israel" (see Micah 5:2; Matthew 2:6).

Herod told the Wise Men to go to Bethlehem and search carefully for the child. When they found Him, he wanted them to come back and tell him so he could go and worship Him too. But Herod did not want to worship the baby like they did—he wanted to kill Him!

The Wise Men left Herod and started on their way to Bethlehem. And then they saw the star again. They were extremely happy because they knew they would see this baby king very soon.

You might think Jesus was still lying in the manger, but that was just when He was born. By the time the Wise Men came to Jesus, Matthew tells us Joseph and Mary were living in a house with Jesus. The Wise Men came in and saw Joseph and Mary and the child Jesus. They opened their treasures and gave Jesus gold, frankincense, and myrrh. When God warned them not to go back to Herod, they went back to their country by a different route. Herod was angry when the Wise Men didn't come back. He decided to kill every baby boy in Bethlehem so he wouldn't lose his kingdom. But Herod was not smarter than God. In a dream, an angel told Joseph to take Jesus and Mary to Egypt because Herod would soon try to kill Him.

They stayed there until an angel told them King Herod the Great was dead and it was safe to take Jesus back to Israel. On the way, Joseph learned Herod's son Archelaus (ark-eh-LAY-us) was ruling over Judea. That made him afraid to take Jesus back to Bethlehem. When God warned him in a dream not to go there, Joseph took Mary and Jesus back to Nazareth. Since Jesus grew up there, most people knew Him as Jesus of Nazareth.

Wouldn't you think everyone would be happy to hear that God's Son was born to be our King? But many people are just like Herod—they want to be their own king or queen. That is really sad because Jesus loves them very much, and He is the only one who can save all of us from our sins and bring us safely to heaven.

LET'S PRAY: Lord God, our heavenly Father, thank You for guiding the Wise Men to Jesus by the Christmas star. Guide me through Your Bible, so I can always be close to Jesus and know that He will always be with me. Amen.

When Jesus is twelve, Mary and Joseph bring Him to the temple. He stays behind, asking questions.

The Boy Jesus in the Temple

If you could go anywhere in the world, where would you go? Why do you want to go there?

Joseph and Mary took little Jesus from Bethlehem and went away to live in Egypt (EE-jipt) because King Herod the Great wanted to kill Jesus (Matthew 2). After Herod died, they returned to Nazareth. Since Jesus grew up there, most people knew Him as Jesus of Nazareth.

It would be fun to read about what kind of a boy Jesus was. What toys did He have? What games did He like to play? What were His friends like? But the Bible tells us only one story from Jesus' childhood, when He was twelve years old.

Like every other year, Joseph took his whole family to Jerusalem for the Feast of the Passover. When Passover had ended, Joseph and Mary started back toward Nazareth, traveling with many families from their town. Jesus wasn't with Joseph and Mary, but they weren't concerned because they thought He was traveling with another family. But at the end of the day, when each family came back together, Jesus was missing. Mary and Joseph searched among their relatives and their friends, but they did not find Him. So with great fear, they rushed back to Jerusalem.

Mary and Joseph searched high and low through the city. They didn't find Him until the third day, when they went back to look in the temple courts. And there He was, sitting with a group of teachers. He was listening to them and asking them questions. They were amazed that a twelve-year-old knew the Scriptures so well.

Mary was upset and asked Jesus, "Son, why have You treated us this way? Behold, Your father and I have been searching for You in great distress." But Jesus asked them, "Why were you looking for Me? Did you not know that I must be in My Father's house?" He was surprised that they didn't think to look for Him at the temple right away. Why didn't they realize that the most important thing in the whole world to Him was talking and learning about God His Father?

If your family was on vacation in a strange city and you wandered off, where would you go? To a shopping mall? a museum? a baseball or football stadium? a park? Or would you go to a church? Jesus knew there is no other place in the whole world as important as the place where we can learn about God and His promises to us. That is why church is so important. That is where we learn about all Jesus did to keep God's promises and save us from our sins. And Sunday School and Bible class are special because there we study the Bible and can ask questions we have about God.

LET'S PRAY: Lord Jesus, thank You for learning God's Word so well and for teaching me how important it is for my faith and my life too. Help me to love reading the Bible all through my life. In Your name. Amen.

Zechariah and Elizabeth's son, John, begins teaching and baptizing at the Jordan River.

John Prepares the Way

What kind of job do you want to have when you grow up?

John the Baptist was living in the wilderness when the word of God came to him. He went into the land around the Jordan River and taught people that they had broken God's Commandments and needed to be baptized to wash their sins away. John wore camel's hair and a leather belt around his waist. Those were the same types of clothes the prophet Elijah had worn.

Large crowds came to John from Jerusalem (jeh-ROO-suh-lem) and Judea to be baptized. But some Pharisees (FAIR-uh-seez) and Sadducees (SAD-joo-seez) came too. These people thought they were so good they didn't need to be baptized. John called them snakes: "You brood of vipers! Who warned you to flee from the wrath to come?" (Matthew 3:7).

He was talking about Judgment Day, when everyone who doesn't believe Jesus is their Savior will be punished in hell. John described them as fruit trees that never bear good fruit. Good fruits are the good things we say and do for our neighbors because we love God and Jesus has saved us. But without God's forgiveness and faith, the things we do and say can never be good. John warned the Pharisees and Sadducees, "Even now the axe is laid to the root of the trees. Every tree therefore that does not bear good fruit is cut down and thrown into the fire" (Matthew 3:10).

The Jewish leaders in Jerusalem sent some people to ask John why he was preaching and baptizing people. They asked if he was the promised Messiah or Elijah the prophet. John said no. Then he used the words of Isaiah and answered, "I am the voice of one crying out in the wilderness, 'Make straight the way of the Lord'" (John 1:23). John was only the messenger for the promised Savior.

That was the most exciting news John had to tell the people. God's promised Savior was here, and soon He would start teaching His people. John said, "I baptize with water, but among you stands one you do not know, even He who comes after me, the strap of whose sandal I am not worthy to untie" (John 1:26–27).

When you grow up, God might lead you to be a pastor or a teacher—or maybe a doctor or a nurse, a police officer or firefighter. Whatever job God leads you to, the most important thing you will ever do is help people see their sin and know that Jesus is their Savior from that sin. When you read your Bible and devotions at home and go to church and Sunday School or Bible class, God is preparing you for that work.

LET'S PRAY: Lord God, thank You for sending John to prepare the way for Jesus. Open my ears to listen to his message and prepare me for Jesus' coming, that I may talk to others about their Savior so they will be ready for His coming too. In Jesus' name. Amen.

John baptizes Jesus. The Holy Spirit flies down as a dove, and God says, "You are My beloved Son."

The Baptism of Jesus

What do you think is so special about being baptized?

When Jesus was all grown up, John the Baptist came and baptized many people along the Jordan River. Then one day, he saw Jesus coming to be baptized too. John was surprised that Jesus came. John's Baptism washed away people's sin—the sin deep inside us that makes us say and do bad things. Deep down inside, John knew he was a sinner too. He needed Jesus to save him like all of us do. But John knew Jesus was God's perfect Son who had no sin to wash away. So John told Jesus, "I need to be baptized by You, and do You come to me?"

Look closely in your Bible at Matthew 3:15 and you will notice Jesus' answer is printed in red. All of His words will be. Jesus told John this was part of God's plan. God the Father sent Jesus into the world to save us from our sin. God sent Him to the Jordan River that day to join His Baptism with ours. In the water of the Jordan, He would take all our sin away from us, put it on His own shoulders, and carry it to the cross, where He would be punished instead of us. After Jesus told John this Baptism was part of God's plan, John agreed and baptized Jesus.

Right away after Jesus was baptized, John watched Him come up out of the water. John saw the heavens torn open like a curtain, and he watched the Holy Spirit come down like a dove and come to rest upon Jesus. That is why Jesus is called *Christ*. The word means "to be anointed," that is, to be set apart by God for an important job. The Holy Spirit would guide Jesus to do everything God His Father wanted Him to do.

Then John heard a loud voice from heaven say, "This is My beloved Son, with whom I am well pleased." That was the voice of God the Father—Jesus' Father—telling John He was very happy with the way Jesus lived His life as a child and a young man. Jesus did it for all of us—so when He took our sin upon Himself in Baptism, He put His holy life on all of us.

Jesus' Baptism makes your Baptism special. When you were baptized, you were joined to Jesus, and Jesus was joined to you. He took away your sin and gave you His perfect life. He made you His own brother or sister, God's own son or daughter. He gave you His Holy Spirit. He made you part of His Church to teach the world about how Jesus saved us by living, dying, and rising to life again.

Because of our Baptism, we are called *Christians*, a word that means "little Christs." God gave us His Holy Spirit to guide us through our lives too. And when you stand before God on Judgment Day, He will see no sin, only Jesus' perfect life. He will be happy to bring you into heaven forever. That is what your Baptism does for you.

LET'S PRAY: Lord God, heavenly Father, thank You for sending Jesus to be baptized and making me Your own child when You baptized me. Give me Your Holy Spirit that I may be ready to tell other people about Your great love. In Jesus' name. Amen.

The Spirit leads Jesus to the desert. The devil tries to trick Jesus to sin. But Jesus doesn't give in.

The Temptation of Jesus

When you are tempted, part of you wants to do something you know is wrong. What temptations are hard for you to say no to?

Right after Jesus was baptized, the Holy Spirit led Him into the wilderness. God the Father wanted to give us a "do-over."

Back in the Garden of Eden, the devil tempted Eve, and both Adam and Eve ate the fruit God commanded them not to eat. Their sin passed on to you and me, making us sinners who should die and receive God's punishment. In this story, Jesus took Adam and Eve's place. If He passed the test without sinning, His obedience would pass on to you and me by faith.

Jesus spent forty days and nights in the wilderness not eating a single thing. At the end, He was really, really hungry. The devil told Him, "If You are the Son of God, command these stones to become loaves of bread."

Do you think part of Jesus was hungry enough to want bread right away? Yes, but using words from the Bible, Jesus answered, "Man shall not live by bread alone, but by every word that comes from the mouth of God." Yes, Jesus was very hungry, but He trusted His heavenly Father to feed Him when the time was right.

Then Satan took Jesus to the top of the temple. He said, "If You are the Son of God, throw Yourself down, for it is written, 'He will command His angels concerning you,' and 'On their hands they will bear you up, lest you strike your foot against a stone.'"

Satan was tricky. If Jesus didn't jump, it would look like He didn't trust His Father's Bible promises!

But Jesus knew that if you really trust God, you never make Him prove He keeps His promises. Using the Bible again, Jesus answered, "Again it is written, 'You shall not put the Lord your God to the test.'"

Finally, Satan took Jesus to a high mountain and showed Him all the kingdoms of the world. Jesus could be king of the whole world if He just bowed down and worshiped Satan.

Do you think part of Jesus might have wanted to do that instead of going to the cross to suffer and die? But Jesus didn't choose the easy way. He answered, "Be gone, Satan! For it is written, 'You shall worship the Lord your God and Him only shall you serve.'"

Since the Son of God commanded him to leave, Satan went away and waited for another time to tempt Him. God the Father sent angels to feed Jesus and take care of Him.

Sometimes, part of you really wants something God doesn't want you to have right now—or maybe ever. Learn the Bible like Jesus did, and the Holy Spirit will give you the strength to say no or wait until God's time is right. But if you fail and sin, like all of us do, remember that Jesus took your sins when He baptized you and paid their price on the cross. Pray to Him, and you will be forgiven.

LET'S PRAY: Lord Jesus, thank You for not giving in to the devil's temptations. Forgive me when I do. Amen.

Jesus calls four fishermen to leave their fishing boats and become His first disciples or followers.

Jesus Calls Four Disciples

If you could go on an adventure, where would you want to go?

After Jesus was baptized, He went up to Galilee (GAL-ih-lee). (Galilee is a region in the northern part of Israel.) It was time to start teaching the people of Israel about God's love and how He had come to save them from their sins.

But Jesus knew His time to preach would be really, really short, only a few years. After He died, rose again, and went back to heaven, how would people like you and me learn about Him? So Jesus chose people to follow Him and learn from Him. We call them disciples. Jesus taught these men so they could lead the Church, write the books of the New Testament, and train people to be pastors and teachers after He returned to heaven.

One day, Jesus was walking along the Sea of Galilee. He met two brothers, Simon Peter and Andrew, who were throwing a net into the sea to go fishing. Jesus told them, "Follow Me, and I will make you fishers of men." Right away, they left their nets and started following Him.

A little farther down the beach, He met two other brothers, James and John. They were sitting in their boat, repairing the nets. Every morning when the fishing was done for the day, fishermen took time to fix their nets so they would be ready for the next catch. Jesus called James and John to follow Him, and they left their father, Zebedee, and his servants in the boat, and they followed Jesus with Peter and Andrew.

This was the start of a tremendous adventure for Peter, Andrew, James, and John. These men would hear Jesus' wonderful words and see His amazing miracles. They would travel with Him all through the land of Israel. They would ride in boats with Him. They would eat and sleep beside Him. They would watch Him die on the cross and rise again. And with the Holy Spirit guiding them, they would write about the things they saw and heard. Those writings are in the New Testament.

When you were baptized, God started you on a wonderful adventure. You may not be able to follow Jesus around like Peter, Andrew, James, and John could. But whenever you read your Bible, you are right there with Jesus and them, listening to His words and seeing the amazing things He did—especially dying on the cross to save you from your sin.

Jesus promised to be right there beside you every day, protecting you from harm and giving you everything you need. He has promised to control everything that happens to you and make it work to bring you closer to Him. And at the end of the adventure, you will be with God your Father and Jesus your Savior forever and ever. What better adventure could you ever hope for?

LET'S PRAY: Lord Jesus, thank You for calling Your first four disciples to leave their lives of fishing and follow You on a great adventure. Thank You for calling me in my Baptism. Forgive my sins, and give me great joy and confidence each day of my adventure through this life toward heaven. In Your name. Amen.

29

Jesus works His first miracle at a wedding. When the wine runs out, He changes water into wine.

Jesus Changes Water into Wine

When you have a big problem, how do you try to solve it?

Early in Jesus' ministry, He was invited to a wedding in a town called Cana. His mother, Mary, had been invited too. Jesus brought along the disciples He had gathered.

Back in those days, wedding celebrations lasted many days. But very early in this party, Mary learned there was a big problem. They had run out of wine. She knew how embarrassed the bride and groom and their families would be if the guests found out. Mary took that problem to Jesus and taught us something very important. She told Jesus, "They have no wine." She didn't tell Jesus how she thought He should solve the problem—she just told Him what the problem was, and then she left it up to Him to decide the best way to take care of it.

Jesus answered, "Woman, what does this have to do with Me? My hour has not yet come." Jesus was looking toward to Good Friday, when He would die on the cross, when He would show the world just how much He loves all people.

Mary trusted Jesus. She told the servants, "Do whatever He tells you."

Jesus told the servants to go fill six large jars clear to the top with water. When the jars were full, Jesus told the servants to draw some out and take it to the master of the feast. The master of the feast was the guy who made sure all the wedding guests had all the food and drink they needed.

The servants did exactly what Jesus said. As they were carrying the water to the master, Jesus used His mighty power to work His first miracle. He turned that water into wine.

When the master of the feast tasted the new wine, he was impressed at how delicious it was. He told the new husband that at most wedding feasts they serve the good wine first. Then, when the guests have been drinking, they bring out wine that is not so good. But he was impressed because this husband saved the best wine for last.

The most amazing thing about this sign, which very few knew about, is that when Jesus had shown His glory, His disciples believed in Him.

With this sign, Jesus directs us (those who hear and read John's account) to His final sign of the cross. So when we call on the Father to help us, the sign of Jesus' death is the proof that He will care for us in every other way. In this way, our Father invites us to pray boldly to Him as dear children ask their fathers. He loves us as a husband dearly loves his bride.

LET'S PRAY: Lord Jesus, thank You for making delicious new wine for the new husband and wife. Remind us that You care about everything in our lives—no matter how big or how small. Help me to teach others about Your great love and kindness. Amen.

Jesus sits down on a mountain and teaches His followers about the kingdom of heaven.

The Sermon on the Mount

How do you think Jesus wants you to treat other children? Why is it hard to do that sometimes?

Jesus went from village to village, telling people about God's love. Large groups of people from all over came to follow Him. One day, they followed Him up onto a mountain, where they all sat down and He began to teach them.

First, He promised forgiveness for those who were sorry for their sins. Jesus said they would live in the new heavens and earth when He came back on Judgment Day. He promised a special blessing to His believers who are treated badly because they love Jesus.

Then Jesus said, "You are the light of the world." That's how we are when we are kind, gentle, and patient with other people. Like a bright light on a dark night, we show that God's love is inside us, and when other people feel that love, some of them will want to know more about Jesus' love.

Next, Jesus talked about the Ten Commandments. Many people think they will go to heaven because they are pretty good and do many good things. But Jesus said being good part of the time isn't good enough for God. We have to be perfect all the time. To show us what He meant, He talked about the commandment "you shall not kill."

Many people think they keep this commandment because they haven't killed anyone. But God looks deep in our hearts and minds. Whenever we hate others and wish they were dead, we break this commandment—even when we hold on to our anger and refuse to forgive them for something bad they did to us. Jesus was teaching us that no matter how hard we try, we are sinners and we will always need His forgiveness, power, and help. So next He taught us how to pray.

Jesus taught us a special prayer we call the Lord's Prayer. It reminds us that God is our Father, who loves us very much. When we pray to Him, we can be sure He will forgive our sins and give us every good thing we really need.

Many people worry they will not have enough food, clothes, or other things to be able to live. Jesus reminds us that God feeds His birds and dresses His flowers to look beautiful—even weeds. He loves us more than birds and plants, so we can be sure He will take care of everything we need.

Jesus ended His sermon with a neat picture. He said if we listen closely and do the things He taught, we will be like a wise person who built his house on a rock. When the rain falls and the wind blows and the water rises, the house will stand strong and secure. But if we don't do what He said, we will be like a foolish person who built his house on sand. When the rain falls, the wind blows, and the water rises, the house will fall with a mighty crash.

LET'S PRAY: Loving Father, thank You for Jesus' wonderful words that teach us how to live. Forgive me when I do wrong, and help me trust You, pray to You, and serve You every way I can. In Jesus' name. Amen.

Jesus is asleep when a storm rises on the lake. He wakes and calms the storm with His words alone.

Jesus Calms a Storm

What kind of weather scares you most?

Jesus went all through Galilee teaching people and healing those who couldn't see, hear, walk, or use their arms. He also healed people who were sick. So many people came to Him that He got really tired, and so did His disciples.

One day, He decided they needed to get away and be by themselves for a little while so they could rest. He got into a boat with all His disciples to go across the Sea of Galilee. Other boats went along with them. Jesus was so tired that He lay down on a cushion in the back of the boat and fell fast asleep.

While He was sleeping, a strong windstorm rose up over the sea. The wind was blowing really hard, and it made the waves grow taller and taller. The waves became so high that they crashed over the side of the boat and started filling it up with water. The disciples watched as the boat sank lower and lower. But when they looked at Jesus, He was sleeping like a baby.

Many of Jesus' disciples were fishermen. They had grown up on this water and had gone through storms before. But this one was really bad. Their boat was filling with water, and they knew it wouldn't be long before it sank. With the huge waves, they didn't think they would be able to swim to the shore when the boat went down. They grew very scared and they woke Jesus, saying, "Teacher, do You not care that we are perishing?"

Jesus woke up and spoke to the wind and sea as if they were children. He commanded them, "Peace! Be still!" Right away, the wind stopped and the sea was completely calm; the waves were gone. Jesus turned to His disciples and asked, "Why are you so afraid? Have you still no faith?"

Everyone on the boat was shocked. Storms just don't stop because a person stands and shouts for them to stop. They said to one another, "Who then is this, that even the wind and the sea obey Him?" More and more, Jesus was showing His disciples He wasn't just a normal man like they were. He was God's Son.

Sometimes, the weather gets bad and we get scared. Lightning, thunder, strong winds, and loud hail are very frightening. Other times, we might get sick, or someone may want to hurt us. But Jesus is the mighty Son of God who created the heavens and the earth. He is in control of the weather and everything that happens on earth. He has promised to take care of us always. And we can trust His promise because He went to the cross to suffer and die for our sins, and He rose to life again on the third day.

LET'S PRAY: Lord Jesus, thank You for showing Your power over the winds and the waves that You created. Whenever I'm scared of storms or other things in my life, remind me that You are in complete control, and I am safe in Your hands. Amen.

Jesus chooses a tax collector named
Matthew to be one of His twelve disciples.

Jesus Calls Matthew Matthew 9:9–13

Is there a bully at your school? Describe what that person is like.

Jesus went through the land of Israel teaching people. One day, He stopped at a tax booth in the road. People had to stop at the booth to pay money to the government when they wanted to sell fish, clothes, or other things to people. It's like the taxes your parents pay when they buy things at the store.

In Jesus' time, people didn't like tax collectors at all. The collectors often took more money than they were supposed to. They were like bullies on a playground—no one could tell them to stop because Roman soldiers stood by them and threatened to beat up anyone who wouldn't pay the taxes.

Matthew was the tax collector sitting at the booth that day. Jesus told him, "Follow Me." Right away, Matthew got up, left the taxes behind, and started following Jesus.

That confused the crowds. They liked Jesus before, but now He was choosing people they hated and inviting them to be His disciples too. They weren't sure how to think about Jesus anymore—should they keep following Him?

Jesus loved them, but He loved the tax collectors too. He wanted to wash away all their sins and give them heaven. He also wanted to change them so they would stop being greedy and selfish and start treating people fairly.

Matthew was so happy, he held a big party for Jesus and the other apostles at his house. His house was filled with tax collectors and other sinners that most people did not like. Together, they had a wonderful time talking to Jesus and learning how much God loved them.

The next day, Matthew left his tax booth behind and followed Jesus as one of the twelve disciples. After Jesus died and rose again, Matthew wrote the very first of the four Gospels, this book that teaches us so much about Jesus. He wrote it especially for the Jews, the people who once hated him for being a tax collector. What kinder thing could he have ever done for them?

Can you imagine Jesus going up to a bully on your playground and telling him He loves him, wants to forgive him, and wants to lead him to heaven? What would you think? What would the other children think who have been beaten up by him? Jesus changes people—even bullies. When they follow Him, He forgives all their sin—even the times they bullied others. He helps them be kind, caring, and helpful.

Do you know how Jesus goes up to bullies and talks to them today? He does it through you and me, when we go up to them and show them God's love and kindness. He does it when we forgive them and treat them nicely. That is very hard to do. It takes God's love and a lot of prayers. But think how wonderful that would be for everyone at your school if the bullies stopped bullying and played nice!

LET'S PRAY: Lord Jesus, thank You for caring about people who get picked on by bullies—and also for caring about the bullies too. Teach me to be kind and loving to everyone—even my bullies—so everyone can see Your love shining like a bright light inside me. Amen.

A twelve-year-old girl gets sick and dies. Jesus goes to her house and makes her alive again.

Jesus Raises Jairus's Daughter

Mark 5:21–24, 35–43

Have you ever been really, really sick?

One day while Jesus was teaching a large crowd, a man named Jairus (JIGH-ruhs) came up to Him. He was very scared and needed Jesus' help very, very badly. He fell on his knees before Jesus and begged Him, "My little daughter is at the point of death. Come and lay Your hands on her, so that she may be made well and live." Jesus and His disciples went with Jairus.

But while they were on their way, some people came from Jairus's house. They told him, "Your daughter is dead. Why trouble the Teacher any further?" When Jesus overheard what they said, He told Jairus, "Do not fear; only believe."

When they got to the house, it was full of people weeping and crying. Jesus asked them why they were carrying on that way. He told them, "The child is not dead but sleeping." But they knew she was dead. They knew that no matter how loudly someone yelled at her or how hard they shook her, she would never wake up. They started laughing at Jesus like He was crazy.

Jesus made them all go outside. Taking along only three of His disciples—Peter, James, and John—Jesus went into the girl's bedroom with Jairus and the girl's mother. Jesus reached out and took hold of the child's hand. He said to her, "Little girl, I say to you, arise."

If Jairus or his wife had tried to do that, she would have stayed dead. But Jesus is the Son of God. When He spoke to her, she immediately sat up, got up out of bed, and started walking around. Jesus told her parents and His three disciples not to tell anyone what had happened. Then He told Jairus and his wife to give her something to eat. Peter, James, and John were amazed and remembered this for a long, long time. In fact, years later when Mark wrote about this miracle, he wrote down the very words Jesus had said to the girl: "Talitha cumi."

Sometimes, girls and boys get really sick. And sometimes, like Jairus's daughter, they even die. But we never have to be afraid of dying, because Jesus died on the cross to take away our sin. He was laid in a tomb, but death was not strong enough to hold the Son of God and keep Him in that tomb. On the third day, Jesus rose from the dead and left the tomb empty.

Death can't hold us, either, because when Jesus comes back on Judgment Day, He will raise up all the dead just as easily as He raised Jairus's daughter. That is why Jesus said the child was not dead but sleeping. That is why the Bible often describes death as sleep—because Jesus will wake us to eternal life when He comes again. Then all of us who trust in Him as our Savior will live with Him forever.

LET'S PRAY: Lord Jesus, thank You for showing us Your power over death. Whenever we are afraid, remind us that You are bigger than any problem we could ever have. Make us ready for the day You return to take us to live with You forever. Amen.

Two blind men ask Jesus to heal them. He takes them away from the crowd and heals their eyes.

Jesus Heals Two Blind Men Matthew 9:27–31

Have you ever prayed for something but God didn't do what you asked?

One day, two blind men followed Jesus around, calling out, "Have mercy on us, Son of David." They believed Jesus was the Messiah, the Savior God had promised to raise up from one of King David's sons.

Today is very different from that time. There are many different kinds of jobs people can do today, even if they can't see. But at the time Jesus lived on earth, there weren't jobs for people who couldn't see, so these men couldn't work to take care of their families and community. There was nothing they could do to make their eyes work. But they believed Jesus could heal them.

Jesus waited to talk to them until they followed Him into the house. He didn't want everyone in the crowd to see this miracle. He turned to them and asked, "Do you believe I am able to do this?" They answered, "Yes, Lord."

Since Jesus is God, He didn't have to wait until they believed in Him before He could heal them. But He wanted them to understand how important their faith was. When Jesus died on the cross, He paid for everyone's sins. But only those who believe in Him will go to heaven. That's how important faith is. So after the blind men told Him they had faith and believed, Jesus touched them and said, "According to your faith be it done to you." Right away, they were able to see.

Of course, they were really, really excited. But Jesus commanded them, "See that no one knows about this." Jesus did not want them to go out and tell everyone that He had healed them. The Jewish people were expecting the Messiah to come and throw out the Roman armies, make Israel free, and make their lives perfect. They did not understand the Old Testament prophets who said the Messiah must suffer and die to take away their sins and make them right with God. Only after He died and rose again would His followers finally understand why He came. Then they would be free to talk about all the miracles they saw.

Jesus taught us two things by healing the blind men. First, He cares very much about things that hurt us and make our lives hard. He won't always solve our problems right away, but He hears our prayers and works for us.

The second thing is how important our faith is. God has the power to do anything we could ever ask—and He cares about us and promises to answer every prayer. The Holy Spirit gives us faith to believe these things about God. But remember one more thing—God is smarter than we are. Sometimes He chooses a better way to answer our prayers than we can think of. When God doesn't do it the way we want, we may feel like He doesn't hear or care. But Jesus' cross proves that is not true. Our God is good, powerful, and loving. He will take care of every problem we will ever have and make everything work for the best.

LET'S PRAY: Lord Jesus, when You healed the two blind men, You showed Your care and kindness for each of us. Give me faith that whenever I have problems and pray to You, You will hear my prayer and do what is best for me. Amen.

Jesus uses five small loaves of bread and two fish to feed a huge crowd of people.

Jesus Feeds Five Thousand

Describe a time you couldn't do something because you were too young or too little.

Jesus and His disciples were very busy. Huge crowds of people kept gathering to hear Him preach and to be healed of their sicknesses. Finally, Jesus told His disciples, "Come away by yourselves to a desolate place and rest awhile." They got on a boat and sailed to the other side of the Sea of Galilee to a place where nobody lived.

But the Sea of Galilee isn't a very big lake. The crowds saw Jesus sail off, so they just walked around the lake to meet Him on the other side. When Jesus and His disciples reached the shore, a huge crowd was waiting for Him!

Jesus looked at their faces, and He knew why they had come. He knew they were hurting and scared. They didn't know if God loved them or if He was going to punish them. So instead of turning around in the boat or ordering the crowds to leave, Jesus welcomed them and began teaching them.

He healed the sick, and He taught and preached all day long. Before the disciples knew it, the sun was getting low in the sky and it was nearly suppertime. They looked around and realized there were no cities on that side of the lake, no places for the people to go and buy food. They urged Jesus to send the crowds away so they could go and find food. But Jesus told them the people didn't need to go away. He said, "You give them something to eat."

The disciples looked at the huge crowd and said, "We only have five loaves here and two fish." That was probably not even enough food for Jesus and the Twelve—it never would have been enough for all those people.

Jesus told them, "Bring the food here to Me." He told the people to sit down in groups on the grass. He took the food, looked up to heaven, and prayed for God His Father to bless it. Then He began handing it to His disciples. They took it from Jesus' hands and started passing it out to the crowds. Jesus kept handing bread and fish to the disciples, and they kept passing it out to the people until everyone was full. Then Jesus told His disciples to gather up all the leftover food so none of it would be wasted. They ended up gathering more leftover food than the five loaves and two fish Jesus started with.

Sometimes, we have to do things that seem too hard. We aren't tall enough, fast enough, smart enough, or strong enough. We don't have enough time or money. But Jesus is able to take what we have and make it more. So whenever you don't know what to do, just look to Jesus and ask Him to help. He'll always be there for you.

LET'S PRAY: Lord Jesus, thank You for reminding us that You will always give us everything we need. Help us to trust You so we can spend our time helping other people instead of worrying about ourselves. Amen.

Jesus walks on the water and gives Peter power to do it too. When Peter is afraid, Jesus saves him.

Jesus Walks on Water

Have you ever had to do something you thought you could never do?

It had been a long, long day for the twelve disciples. After Jesus spent all day teaching, He fed a huge crowd with a little bread and a few fish. Then while He stayed back to send the crowds home and pray, He made the disciples get in a boat and row to the other side of the sea. But they were having a tough time because the wind was blowing hard against them. They had been rowing most of the night, but they still hadn't reached the other shore.

Suddenly, they saw something that scared them to death. Someone or something was walking across the water right at them! They cried out in fear, "It is a ghost!"

But it wasn't a ghost—it was Jesus! He told them, "Take heart; it is I. Do not be afraid." He was right there—the Son of God was walking across the top of the water toward them! Their fear turned to happiness. Peter said, "Lord, if it is You, command me to come to You on the water." Peter knew he couldn't walk on water by himself—but Jesus could give him the power to do it. Jesus told him, "Come."

Peter stood up, stepped over the side of the boat and down onto the water, and it worked—the water held him up! He took a few steps and sure enough, the water held firm under him just like he was walking across the ground. He started walking to Jesus.

But then Peter looked around. He felt the wind blowing, saw the waves, and got scared. He remembered that people can't walk on water, and as his faith got replaced by doubt and fear, he quickly sank into the waves. Looking to Jesus, he cried out, "Lord, save me." Right away, Jesus reached out and took him by the hand. He pulled Peter back on top of the water and said, "O you of little faith, why did you doubt?"

Peter held tight to Jesus' hand, and they walked together to the boat.

When they got into the boat, the winds stopped blowing. The twelve disciples in the boat were shocked and amazed. They bowed and fell down at Jesus' feet and said, "Truly You are the Son of God."

Sometimes we have to do really hard things, things that seem impossible, like maybe trying to figure out something new in math, going to the hospital for a scary surgery, or going out to the playground where someone is being really mean. But Jesus is always right here with us, and nothing is too hard for Him. He has the power to help us do anything we need to do. And the good news is that even when we have doubts and get really scared, Jesus is right there, reaching out to hold us safely in His strong hand. He can pick us back up and keep us safe while He walks with us through our problems and worries.

LET'S PRAY: Lord Jesus, thank You for being there for Peter when he started doubting. Thank You for being there for me when I get scared. Make my faith strong to know You will always be here for me. Amen.

45

Many sick people come to Jesus, and He heals each and every one.

Jesus Heals Many

Have you ever gone to the doctor's office and looked around at the people sitting in the waiting room? What clues could help you guess what is hurting them?

In the Gospels, the books about Jesus' life on earth, we read many times where Jesus healed a blind man or a deaf person, raised a dead girl to life again, or drove a demon out of a boy. It is easy to think that Jesus healed only a few people at a time, here or there. But the Gospels tell us about times when huge crowds came to Jesus bringing many, many people who were sick and hurting—and Jesus healed them all.

One of those times happened when Jesus was walking along the Sea of Galilee. Matthew tells us what he saw: "Great crowds came to Him, bringing with them the lame, the blind, the crippled, the mute, and many others, and they put them at His feet, and He healed them."

Lame people are people who are too weak to walk. Blind people cannot see. Crippled people have weak or bent arms or legs and can't walk or do things with their hands. Mute people are unable to talk.

The crowds brought these sick people to Jesus because they had heard how He had healed sick people in other towns. And Jesus healed every single person who was brought to Him. And this didn't happen just once—it happened many, many times during His ministry, when He went around teaching about God's kingdom before He died on the cross.

We read in the Old Testament about how God worked through prophets to heal a few people—especially through the prophets Elijah and Elisha. But Jesus was healing great crowds of people in many different places! This is exactly what God's Old Testament prophets said the Messiah would do when He came. All these healing miracles made it clear that Jesus was that Messiah, whom God had promised

to Adam and Eve. When the crowds saw Jesus healing everyone who came to Him, they were amazed and said great things about God.

When you get sick and see the doctor, most times you don't feel good right away. The doctor may give you some pills, but sometimes it takes a few days before you start feeling better. Some children have to have surgery where the doctor goes in and fixes something in their bodies that isn't working right. That takes even longer to feel better.

But when people came to Jesus, He made them feel good right away—no medicine, no surgery. Remember, Jesus didn't come just to heal sick bodies, though. He came to take away our sins on the cross and to save us from hell. When you were baptized, He took your sins away and promised you eternal life with Him in heaven. When He comes again, He will heal our bodies perfectly, all at once. Then we will live with Jesus forever, never ever to get sick again.

LET'S PRAY: Lord Jesus, thank You for caring about all the people who came to You and healing so many who were sick. When my body isn't working right and I don't feel well, remind me that You are here. And when You return, You will make my body perfect forever. Amen.

Jesus goes back to teach in His hometown, Nazareth. The people get angry and try to kill Him.

Jesus Is Rejected at Nazareth Luke 4:16–30

What are some Bible stories you've heard over and over again?

After Jesus was baptized, He went through the towns in Galilee doing many mighty miracles—healing people who were hurting, raising the dead, even driving out demons. The news spread, and people came from all the nearby towns to hear Him and see Him. Now, it was time for Jesus to go back home to Nazareth, the town where He grew up and worked in Joseph's carpenter shop.

The people of Nazareth had heard about all the wonderful things Jesus was doing. They invited Him to come and speak in their synagogue (SINN-uh-gog), their church. So Jesus stood up to read from Isaiah. He read, "The Spirit of the Lord is upon Me, because He has anointed Me to proclaim good news to the poor. He has sent Me to proclaim liberty to the captives and recovering of sight to the blind, to set free those who are oppressed, to proclaim the year of the Lord's favor."

Jesus started to preach and said, "Today this Scripture has been fulfilled in your hearing." He told His friends and neighbors that He was the Savior God had promised to send them.

At first, the people of Nazareth were excited to listen to the wonderful things Jesus was saying, and they really respected Him. But then they started thinking about all those years Jesus had lived there as a boy and a young man. They had never seen Him heal someone who was sick or drive out a demon or raise someone who was dead. They only saw Him working in Joseph's carpenter shop or sweeping the floor at the end of the day. They got mad and refused to believe He could be the promised Savior.

Jesus heard them grumbling against Him, and He told them they were as stubborn as the people in Elijah and Elisha's time. Since so many Israelites had refused to believe Elijah and Elisha, God did not let the prophets do miracles for many Israelites, but mostly for some Gentile neighbors.

When Jesus told the people of Nazareth He was not going to heal their sick, that really made them mad. They grabbed Him and carried Him to a very high cliff on the edge of their town. They were going to throw Him off the cliff to kill Him. But Jesus used His mighty power to pass right through them, and He went away.

When you grow up going to church, you hear the same stories of things Jesus said and did many, many times, over and over again. When you get older, it can be easy to think, "Oh, I've heard that before," and then stop listening and paying attention—and in time, stop believing in Jesus. That is why we need to listen very closely whenever we hear or read the stories about Jesus' life, His death, and His resurrection. That is why we pray to the Holy Spirit to keep us believing and loving Jesus, our Savior.

LET'S PRAY: Jesus, it is sad when people get so used to hearing about You that they stop noticing how great, kind, and wonderful You are. Help me never get tired of hearing about You. Make my faith strong and alive every day of my life. Amen.

Jesus meets a man who has many demons living in him. Jesus forces the demons out of him.

Jesus Drives Out Demons

Luke 8:26–39

What do you think a demon is like?

Once, Jesus sailed across the Sea of Galilee in a boat with His disciples. When He got out on the other side, He was met by a man who had a demon.

Demons are bad angels who hate God and hate us. They weren't that way when God first created them. At first, they were all good and holy and kind. So was their leader, the angel we now call the devil. But that powerful angel turned against God and convinced a lot of angels to join him against God. We call these bad, fallen angels demons.

The demon inside this man made him very dangerous, so the rulers put him in chains. But the demon made the man so strong that he broke the chains, and no one could control him. The demon made him live far away from other people—he stayed in the places where dead people were buried. Everyone was so afraid they stayed far away from him.

When Jesus landed, the demon made the man come up to Him and shout as loudly as he could, "What have You to do with me, Jesus, Son of the Most High God? I beg You not to torment me." These really bad angels knew the Son of God, and they were afraid of Him. They knew Jesus had come to earth to destroy their works. They knew that one day God would punish them for all the bad things they had done.

Jesus asked the demon his name, and it said "Legion." This was the name the Roman army gave to a group of four thousand to six thousand soldiers, so there were thousands of demons living together inside this man. Jesus commanded them to leave the man. They begged Him to let them go into a herd of pigs that was feeding nearby. Jesus let them go. The demons entered the pigs and made them all rush off the cliff into the Sea of Galilee, where they all died. This scared the people of that land, and they begged Jesus to leave them. So He got ready to get back in the boat and sail over to the other side.

The man was now free of the demons. He came up to thank Jesus and asked if he could follow Him. Instead, Jesus told him to stay and tell his neighbors everything God had done for him. He obeyed Jesus, and his neighbors were amazed when they heard about Jesus driving out all those demons.

The devil and his bad angels can be very scary—until we realize how much stronger Jesus is. When He died on the cross, He set us free from their tricks and their power. When He returns again, He will send them to hell forever, and they will never escape to tempt us or bother us ever again. Until then, He sends us holy angels to guard and protect us, so we don't ever have to be afraid the devil or his demons will come into us and take control.

LET'S PRAY: Lord Jesus, even the bad angels have to obey You when You give them commands. Take away any fear I have of them, so I can trust You and show Your love to the people around me. Amen.

51

Jesus tells a story of a man badly hurt by robbers.
A kind Samaritan saved the man. Jesus saved us.

The Good Samaritan

Which kids at school are the hardest for you to be nice to? Why?

Many Jewish teachers were telling people the only way they could get to heaven was to carefully follow a list of rules or laws the teachers had made up. That is why they were called "lawyers." One of these lawyers asked Jesus what a person had to do to get into heaven.

Jesus asked him, "What is written in the Law? How do you read it?" Jesus was talking about God's Ten Commandments.

The lawyer answered, "You shall love the Lord your God with all your heart and with all your soul and with all your strength and with all your mind, and your neighbor as yourself." These are God's words that show how to keep His Ten Commandments.

Jesus told him, "You have answered correctly; do this, and you will live."

The teacher was proud. Maybe he didn't love all people as much as he loved himself, but if only certain people counted as his neighbor, he could certainly get into heaven on his own. He asked Jesus, "Who is my neighbor?"

So Jesus told a story about a Jewish man who was walking down the road from Jerusalem to Jericho. Thieves beat him, stole his clothes and possessions, and left him half dead. This poor man was going to die unless someone stopped and helped him.

Two Jewish leaders went by—a priest and a Levite. Both of them saw the beaten man, but they walked to the other side of the road and passed by like they had never seen him. Then a Samaritan came along. The Jews hated the Samaritans and treated them badly. But when this Samaritan looked at the dying Jewish man, he felt sorry for him, and he stopped to take care of him.

Jesus asked the teacher, "Which of these three, do you think, proved to be a neighbor to the man?" The teacher said it was the Samaritan because he stopped to take care of him. Jesus told him to go and do the same: Treat every single person as if he or she were his neighbor—even people he didn't like and people who didn't like him.

Some people hear this parable of the Good Samaritan and think Jesus was teaching that if we just love people and treat everyone like our neighbor, we can get to heaven without faith in Him. But He was showing that none of us keeps God's rules. None of us loves God more than everything else, and none of us loves every other person as much as we love ourselves. Think about the boy or girl at school who picks on you or makes fun of you. Do you love him or her as much as you love yourself? The only way we can be saved is by trusting in Jesus, who loved every one of us enough to take our sins and die on the cross in our place.

LET'S PRAY: Lord Jesus, I can't keep all of God's Commandments perfectly. Thank You for coming to earth to keep those rules for me and for dying on the cross to take away the punishment I deserve for breaking them. Amen.

53

Jesus' disciples asked Him to teach them how to pray. He taught us to pray the Lord's Prayer.

How would you teach a friend to pray?

Jesus prayed a lot. He prayed when He woke up in the morning, before and after He ate, and when He went to bed. Jesus got up early some mornings to pray—and stayed up really late some nights. Sometimes, He never went to bed at all because He was praying.

The disciples asked Jesus, "Lord, teach us to pray." Jesus taught them a special prayer, a prayer we use in church every single week, a prayer you should pray every day. It goes like this:

Our Father who art in heaven. God made you His own son or daughter when He baptized you. Since He is in heaven, He can give you everything you could ask for.

Hallowed be Thy name. Hallowed means "holy," and God's name is His reputation—what people think about Him. We ask God to help us trust that He is good and perfect—and to help us teach that to others.

Thy kingdom come. God is our King. When Jesus comes back, He will send away everyone that refuses to serve Him and believe in Him. We ask Him to make us ready for that day by faith, and to help us warn others so they will believe in Jesus and always be ready.

Thy will be done on earth as it is in heaven. In heaven, the holy angels always do everything God tells them to do. We thank God for saving us through Jesus, and we ask Him to help us love Him and all other people as He wants.

Give us this day our daily bread. Jesus teaches us to ask God for our food, clothes, family, friends, and everything we need to live.

And forgive us our trespasses as we forgive those who trespass against us. We ask God to forgive us for Jesus' sake for the times we break His rules. We ask God to help us forgive people who sin against us.

And lead us not into temptation. The devil, people around us, and our own sinful nature tempt us to do bad things. We ask God to help us say no and do what God wants.

But deliver us from evil. We ask God to protect us from the devil's plans and keep our faith strong so we will always believe in Jesus and be ready for Him to come again.

That was the end of the prayer Jesus taught His disciples. In church, we add a few more words at the end to thank Jesus and to remind us God will always answer our prayers:

For Thine is the kingdom and the power and the glory, forever and ever. Amen. God is our great King who has the power to do everything we need. The word "Amen" says we believe God will answer our prayers for Jesus' sake.

In this great prayer, Jesus gives us just the right words to pray to God our Father so we can be sure He will give us what we need, all for Jesus' sake. Amen.

LET'S PRAY: Lord Jesus, thank You for Your wonderful prayer. Remind me that You always hear me and that Your Father loves me as His own child. Then I can pray and know that You will give me what is best. Amen.

In Jesus' story, a young man made his father sad,
but when he came home, his father forgave him.

The Prodigal Son

How do you feel about the children at school who break the rules and get into trouble a lot?

Jewish lawyers taught people they had to keep rules to get to heaven. The Pharisees were people who looked up to these lawyers and tried to keep all their rules.

Most Pharisees were proud of themselves and hated people who broke the rules. They thought tax collectors and sinners would never go to heaven. So when they saw Jesus eating and drinking with these rule breakers, they grumbled and complained.

Jesus told them a story about a dad who had two sons. The younger son asked his dad to give him a lot of money. Then he moved far away where he could break his father's rules and do whatever he wanted. He spent all that money doing bad things. But when his money was gone, things turned really bad. He had no job, no food, no home, no friends. The only work he could find was feeding food scraps to pigs. He was so hungry, he would have eaten those nasty, stinky scraps—but no one cared or gave him anything.

Then he started thinking about home. He thought of how hungry he was, and how his father's servants had more than enough to eat. Knowing he didn't deserve to be treated like a son anymore, he decided to go home, tell his dad he was wrong, and ask if he could become one of the servants.

But when his dad saw him walking home, he loved him and ran out to him. He hugged him, put new clothes on him, and had a big feast to welcome him home—not as a servant, but as his son.

The older brother heard about it, and he was upset. Like the Pharisees seeing Jesus eating with the rule breakers who came back to God, he refused to join the celebration. So the father went out and begged him to come in. But the older son complained that he always kept his father's rules and never disobeyed, but he was never given a meal to celebrate with his friends.

The problem was the older son didn't really know his father at all. He thought he was a mean dad who only loved his children if they kept all the rules. But a good father does not love his children like that. He loves them no matter what—even if they break the rules. Since the younger son returned to his father and confessed his sins, it was right to welcome him back as a full son and celebrate.

It is easy for us to be proud and think we are better than boys and girls who break the rules. But we break God's rules when we sin. Still, God our Father loves us—and He loves them too. Jesus came to suffer and die for them just like He came to suffer and die for us. God wants us to go and tell them He loves them and wants to bring them home to heaven too.

LET'S PRAY: Lord Jesus, teach me to love all boys and girls, even the ones who break all the rules and make my life hard. Teach me what to say to show them Your love and goodness. Amen.

Ten sick men ask Jesus for help. After He heals all ten, only one comes back to thank Him.

Jesus Heals Ten Lepers

Luke 17:11–19

Have you ever wanted something very, very much for your birthday or Christmas?

esus was traveling to Jerusalem. He entered a village and was met by ten lepers. Leprosy was a terrible disease that easily passed from one person to the next. To stop it from spreading as quickly, God required lepers to stay far away from other people. People with leprosy had to leave their villages and towns. Since they could no longer be with their families and friends, lepers often lived together, like these ten.

The lepers stood far away from Jesus and in loud voices called out, "Jesus, Master, have mercy on us." To "have mercy" means to care so much about someone who is suffering that you have to do something to help. Sometimes when Jesus met lepers, He showed His mercy by walking up to them, touching them, and healing them. But this time, Jesus stayed where He was and told them, "Go and show yourselves to the priests." They did what Jesus said and went on their way. While they were going, Jesus healed their leprosy, and they were healthy again.

Nine of the ten were so excited they forgot all about Jesus. Maybe they thought about their families and friends and how wonderful it was going to be to run back and touch them again. Maybe they thought about all the things they could do now that they were healthy again. These nine hurried off and forgot all about Jesus, who had given them back their lives.

But one remembered. He came running back, fell on his face at Jesus' feet, and thanked Him over and over and over again. And the strange thing was that this man was not a Jew like the other nine. He was a Samaritan.

Jesus was happy that he had come back, but He asked about the nine Jews. He said, "Were not ten cleansed? Where are the other nine?

Was no one found to return and give praise to God except this foreigner?" Then He turned to the Samaritan and said, "Rise and go your way; your faith has made you well."

Think about that birthday or Christmas present you had been wanting and waiting for so long. What did you do when you got it? Did you open it up and start playing with it? Did you ever think about the person who gave it to you, stop playing, and say thank you? Many times in your life, God will give you great things. Saying thank You in a prayer will help you remember how good God is to give you so many good things every day.

But sometimes bad things happen—like when you get sick, lose friends, have to move, get hurt or scared or worried. That's when it is good to remember to pray to Jesus to help you. But what happens after He helps you and takes that problem away? Then we need to remember to stop and thank Him for helping us.

LET'S PRAY: Heavenly Father, You have been so good and kind to me and to all people. Forgive me for not always remembering to stop and thank You for all Your kindness to me. Now and each time You answer my prayers, remind me to stop and give You thanks. In Jesus' name. Amen.

A leader named Nicodemus comes to visit Jesus.
Jesus teaches him about Baptism and God's love.

Why is it important to follow rules?

Pharisees were not full-time church workers like the priests and Levites. They were normal Jews who thought they could gain entrance to God's heavenly home if they were careful to follow all the rules their teachers taught them. Jesus came along and taught them that it did not make God happy when they trusted in their rule-keeping rather than in His love for them. Many of the Pharisees were upset at this and refused to listen to Him.

But some Pharisees listened to Jesus. One was Nicodemus (nick-uh-DEE-muhs), an important Jewish leader and a judge on the highest Jewish court. All the miracles made him believe Jesus was from God. He wanted to talk to Jesus but was scared he would get in trouble if the other judges and leaders saw him with Jesus. So he waited until it was dark outside.

One night, Nicodemus came and told Jesus, "We know You are a teacher come from God, for no one can do these signs that You do unless God is with Him." Jesus answered him, "Truly, truly I say to you, unless one is born again he cannot see the kingdom of God."

Nicodemus tried really hard, but he couldn't understand what Jesus meant when He said one must be "born again." He asked, "How can a man be born when he is old?" Did Jesus mean he had to go back in his mom's tummy and be born a second time?

Jesus answered, "Unless one is born of water and the Spirit, he cannot enter the kingdom of God." Now it was clear. Jesus was talking about God making people new again, as He does in Baptism. Most Pharisees had refused to be baptized. They knew Baptism was to wash away sins. But they didn't think they had any sins to wash away; they thought they were good people who did not need God's work on them.

Jesus told Nicodemus, "What is born of the flesh is flesh, and what is born of the Spirit is spirit." He meant that the first time we were born, we had the same sinful nature our mothers and fathers have. No matter how hard we try to keep the rules, we are not good enough. We all need to have our sins washed away.

Jesus told Nicodemus what gives Baptism its power to wash away sins: "For God so loved the world, that He gave His only Son, that whoever believes in Him should not perish but have eternal life."

Nicodemus was used to following rules. Rules are a good thing when they help us get along with other people and treat one another fairly. But rules can't make us right with God. Only Jesus can do that. God loved each of us so much, He sent Jesus, His Son, to keep the Commandments for us. Then, He punished Jesus on the cross for all the times we break His rules. In Baptism, God washed away your sins and made you His own child for Jesus' sake. Because of Jesus' perfect life, His death on the cross, and His resurrection, you have life with our heavenly Father right now; and you will see God in His own house.

LET'S PRAY: Lord Jesus, thank You for my Baptism, when the Holy Spirit gave me a new birth as God's own child. Thank You for forgiving my sin. Help me to live as God's child, sharing the story of Your love with everyone I meet. Amen.

Tired and thirsty, Jesus meets a woman by a well.
He teaches her about God's love and forgiveness.

Jesus and the Samaritan Woman John 4:1–45

What would you do if a new child came to school who was really different from everyone else?

Jesus did most of His teaching in the land called Galilee. But when there were big festivals like Passover, Jesus led His disciples south from Galilee down to the temple, in the land called Judea. But between Galilee and Judea was a land called Samaria. The people who lived there were called Samaritans.

The Jews hated the Samaritans very much, but Jesus didn't. One day when He was traveling through Samaria with His disciples, they entered a Samaritan village around noon. Jesus and His disciples were tired, hungry, and thirsty. So He sent them off to buy food while He sat down by the well to rest.

When a Samaritan woman came to the well, Jesus said, "Give Me a drink."

She looked at Him in surprise and asked why He would want water from her, since Jews hated Samaritans.

Jesus said He would give her living water if she asked Him. Pointing to the well, He said, "Everyone who drinks of this water will be thirsty again, but whoever drinks of the water that I will give him will never be thirsty again." Jesus was teaching her about faith, but she thought He meant actual water. She asked Him to give her that water so she could stop coming to the well.

Jesus said, "Go, call your husband, and come here." The woman answered, "I have no husband." Jesus already knew that. He said, "You are right in saying, 'I have no husband'; for you have had five husbands, and the one you now have is not your husband. What you have said is true."

The woman was amazed Jesus knew all about her. He had never met her before. She told Him she thought He was a prophet. She talked with Jesus about the difference between the ways Jews and Samaritans worshiped God. Jesus told her those differences didn't really matter at all to God. God is a spirit who cares more about faith in our hearts than where we worship Him. She mentioned one thing that both Jews and Samaritans had in common— both groups believed that God's promised Savior was coming, and both were looking forward to meeting Him.

Jesus told her, "I am He."

The woman believed. She was so excited she ran off and told her neighbors, "Come, see a man who told me all that I ever did. Can this be the Christ?"

Many Samaritans heard what she said, and they believed in Jesus. They came and asked Jesus to stay with them. When He stayed and talked with them two extra days, many more Samaritans believed in Him.

Sometimes, it's scary to meet someone who is different from us. But maybe you can think how scary it is to be in a new place where you don't know anyone! This is a great time to be a good friend and tell others all about Jesus' love and forgiveness.

LET'S PRAY: Lord Jesus, thank You for showing me the way to talk to someone who is different from me. Fill my heart with love for all people—especially those who need to hear about Your love. Amen.

Jesus meets a man who can't walk. Jesus makes
the man's legs strong so he can walk again.

Jesus Heals a Man Who Can't Walk

Have you ever met someone who couldn't walk? What are some things you couldn't do anymore if you couldn't walk?

The Bible tells us that Jesus healed people who were blind or deaf or had leprosy. In this reading, Jesus healed a man who was not able to walk. It happened in Jerusalem.

This man was lying by a pool called Bethesda (buh-THEZ-duh). He was with a large group of people who were blind, lame, or paralyzed. Since these people couldn't see or move around well, they weren't able to work or hold jobs. So they gathered here by this pool.

They were here because they had heard stories that God sent an angel to this pool from time to time. When the water got stirred up, everyone made their way to the water as fast as they could go, and whoever was the first person to get into the water was supposed to be healed.

Jesus came through the courtyard and saw this man. He knew that he had been there a long, long time. Jesus asked him, "Do you want to be healed?"

The man answered, "Sir, I have no one to put me into the pool when the water is stirred up, and while I am going another steps down before me."

Jesus told him, "Get up, take your bed, and walk." And by the power of His words, Jesus healed the man right away. He got up on his feet, picked up his bed, and started walking. Some Jews saw the man carrying his bed, and they asked him why he was breaking the rules, carrying a load on the Sabbath Day.

The man answered, "The man who healed me, that man said to me, 'Take up your bed, and walk.'" They asked who healed him, but he didn't know. Jesus had disappeared into the crowds.

A little later that day, Jesus found the man in the temple and told him, "See, you are well! Sin no more, that nothing worse may happen to you."

The man went away and told the Jews that Jesus was the man who had healed him and told him to carry his bed. That made some of the Jewish leaders really mad at Jesus. They thought He was breaking the Sabbath rules by working all these miracles. They tried to argue with Him and treat Him in a very mean way.

Jesus told them that God His Father always takes care of His children, and Jesus does too.

This made the Jews even more angry. Jesus wasn't just breaking their Sabbath rules. When He called God His own Father, He was making Himself equal to God. They clearly understood that Jesus was claiming to be God's Son, but they didn't want to believe that to be true.

Jesus did such tremendous things to help people who were hurting—like this man who couldn't walk. Healing this man was another sign that showed that Jesus is the Christ, and people should believe in Him to have a new life.

LET'S PRAY: Lord Jesus, thank You for healing the man so he could get up and walk. Keep me strong in faith so no sin will keep me from You. Amen.

Jesus says that He is our Good Shepherd. He loves us so much, He will die to protect us.

The Good Shepherd

What is your favorite animal? What do you like about it?

Long ago, David wrote beautiful Psalm 23, where he compared himself to a sheep. For many years, he had been a shepherd keeping watch over the sheep of his father, Jesse. He realized God watches over us like a shepherd. So he started writing, "The LORD is my shepherd" (Psalm 23:1). In the tenth chapter of John, Jesus said, "I am the good shepherd."

To understand what Jesus was saying, we need to know a little bit about sheep. Sheep are not strong animals. They are not extra fast, and they don't have a lot of ways to defend themselves. If a wolf attacks a herd of unprotected sheep, it has an easy time grabbing one. Also, sheep easily wander off from one another in search of food to eat. It is easy for them to get lost and hurt.

So a shepherd has a very important job. He has to watch his sheep carefully and always be ready to keep them safe, remembering that many wild animals are hunting after them.

When Jesus said, "I am the good shepherd," He was reminding us of how much we need Him. Like sheep and lambs, we can't see the wolves that are hiding in the tall grass, sneaking up to grab us. The devil, the sinful people around us, and our own sinful desires put us in great danger. But Jesus knows they are there. He is keeping watch over them—and using His Bible and His gifts to protect us from them.

When David offered to fight the giant Goliath, King Saul wasn't sure. David was a young man and Goliath a skilled soldier. But David told him about things he had done when he was a shepherd: "When there came a lion, or a bear, and took a lamb from the flock, I went after him and struck him and delivered it out of his mouth. And if he arose against me, I caught him by his beard and struck him and killed him" (1 Samuel 17:34–35).

That is the greatest thing about Jesus, our Good Shepherd. Each of us was trapped, and the devil had us in great danger. But Jesus didn't leave us. He went to the cross to suffer and die to save us. But He didn't stay dead—a dead shepherd can't help the sheep anymore. No, Jesus rose again, so He will always be our Good Shepherd, protecting us and leading us to heaven.

There are many scary things in this world, but we don't have to be afraid, because Jesus is protecting us and guiding us through life. It's nice to know Jesus is always there. But not every boy and girl knows it. Jesus has given us the happy job of telling others that they have someone watching over them. Jesus wants to protect everyone from every harm and danger and lead them home to heaven.

LET'S PRAY: Lord Jesus, thank You for laying down Your life to save me from the devil, sin, and death. Thank You also for rising to life again on the third day. Because You are my living Good Shepherd, I don't ever need to be afraid. Amen.

Jesus' friend Lazarus gets sick, dies, and is buried.
Jesus goes to his grave and raises him to life.

Jesus Raises Lazarus John 11:1–44

How does it feel when someone you love dies?

Jesus had many good friends beyond His twelve disciples. Three of the closest were two sisters and their brother—Mary, Martha, and Lazarus. They lived in a little village outside of Jerusalem called Bethany.

While Jesus was teaching in Galilee, the sisters sent Him a message that Lazarus was very, very sick. But Jesus told His disciples Lazarus's sickness would not end in death, and He stayed in Galilee two more days.

In Bethany, the sisters stayed at Lazarus's side, waiting for Jesus to come. They watched their brother get sicker and sicker, but Jesus never showed up. Finally, Lazarus died.

On the third day, Jesus told His disciples, "Let us go to Judea again. Our friend Lazarus has fallen asleep, but I go to awaken him." The disciples said, "Lord, if he has fallen asleep, he will recover." Jesus answered, "Lazarus has died, and for your sake I am glad that I was not there, so that you may believe. But let us go to him."

After Lazarus had been buried four days, Martha heard Jesus was coming. She met Him and said, "Lord, if You had been here my brother would not have died. But even now I know that whatever You ask from God, God will give You."

Jesus told her, "Your brother will rise again." Martha said, "I know that he will rise again in the resurrection on the last day." But Jesus answered, "I am the resurrection and the life." He explained that if a person believes in Him, that person will live, even though his or her body may die. And everyone who lives and believes in Him will never suffer the death of their soul in hell. They will instead experience joy and peace in God's presence.

Martha went in and told her sister Mary, "The Teacher is here and is calling for you." Mary came out, but she was so upset all she could say was, "Lord, if You had been here, my brother would not have died."

Jesus asked where Lazarus's tomb was, and they said, "Lord, come and see." And Jesus cried.

He followed them to the tomb; then, He told them to roll away the stone. After praying to His Father, Jesus called out in a loud voice, "Lazarus, come out!" The dead man came out, all wrapped in cloth. Jesus told them to untie him and let him go.

After Jesus died on the cross, He was wrapped in cloths and laid in a tomb with a big stone rolled in front of it. On the third day, the angel came down and rolled the stone away from the empty tomb to show Jesus had risen from the dead.

If you have had to bury someone you love, you know the pain Martha and Mary felt. But Jesus is the resurrection and the life. He will return on Judgment Day to raise the people we love who died believing in Him. Then, we will live together with them in God's heavenly home forever.

LET'S PRAY: Lord Jesus, thank You for showing Your power over death by raising Lazarus—but first showing us by Your tears how much You care about us and the hurts we feel. Give me such faith in Your resurrection that I may always find joy and hope, even when someone I love very much dies. Amen.

High on a mountain, three disciples see Jesus'
body shining brightly, showing He is God's Son.

The Transfiguration

What is the most amazing thing you have ever seen?

Peter, James, and John saw Jesus do some amazing things—like healing sick people and walking on water. But on one special night, they saw something even more amazing.

Jesus and these three disciples climbed up a high mountain together. Near the top, Jesus began to pray while the three fell asleep (see Luke 9:32). Suddenly, a bright light startled them. But it was not the moon or the sun—it was Jesus! His face was shining brighter than the sun! His body was shining so brightly it made the clothes He was wearing look dazzling white—like snow on a sunny day that is so bright it makes you squint your eyes.

Peter, James, and John had trouble waking up, but they knew Jesus wasn't alone. Moses and Elijah were standing with Him, and they were shining too! The Old Testament men were talking about Jesus' exodus—something He would do at Jerusalem.

The three disciples didn't understand yet, but Moses and Elijah were talking about how Jesus would die on the cross outside Jerusalem. He would be the Passover Lamb, whose blood is placed on us in our Baptism, so the angel of death will pass over us. Like Moses led the people of Israel out of slavery in Egypt, Jesus will bring us out of slavery to sin and hell and lead us to our promised home in heaven.

At that point, the disciples were wide awake. They saw Moses and Elijah turning to leave. Peter wanted them to stay, so he said, "Lord, it is good that we are here. If You wish, I will make three tents here, one for You and one for Moses and one for Elijah." While Peter was talking, a bright cloud came down and covered them. From the cloud, they heard a voice say, "This is My beloved Son, with whom I am well pleased; listen to Him."

The three disciples were terribly frightened. They fell down on their faces and didn't move until Jesus bent down and touched them. He said, "Rise, and have no fear." They looked up and saw no one was there except Jesus—and He wasn't shining anymore. He looked just the same as before.

As Jesus led them back down the mountain, He told them not to tell anyone else what they had seen. Not until He would rise from the dead.

We call this event Jesus' transfiguration (trans-fig-yur-AY-shuhn). This word talks about something that morphs or changes. With their own eyes, Peter, James, and John saw that Jesus is not only human, but He is also God's almighty Son.

One day, you and I will see Jesus shining in this same beautiful glory forever and ever. Like Moses and Elijah, we will be able to talk with Him and thank Him for saving us. But then that amazing sight will never end—we will be able to see Jesus in all His beautiful brightness and dazzling light forever and ever.

LET'S PRAY: Lord Jesus, I can't wait to see You shining in glory with my own eyes. Until then, help me share Your story with all my family and friends, so they can live with You and see Your glory too. Amen.

When parents bring their children to Jesus, His disciples try to stop them, but Jesus welcomes the children.

Jesus Blesses the Little Children

What are some things grown-ups have done that made you feel special?

J esus loved people very much. He healed those who were sick; He ate and drank with tax collectors and sinners nobody else loved; and He forgave people who felt really bad about things they shouldn't have done. But Jesus also showed His love for another group—little children like you.

Not everyone loves to have children around. Some grown-ups think children are too noisy, too silly, and too much trouble.

Jesus' disciples got upset when they saw parents bringing their little children to Jesus. These moms and dads wanted Jesus to touch their boys and girls and bless them. But the disciples wouldn't let them see Jesus. They sent them away.

Jesus was not happy when He saw this. He told His disciples to let the little children come to Him and not to stand in their way. He told them that God's kingdom belonged to little children. In fact, they would not even see heaven unless they received God's kingdom the way little children do (see Mark 10:15).

What did He mean? Grown-ups work hard to earn money to pay for houses, cars, clothes, and food for their children. Sometimes, all that work makes grown-ups think they are doing it all, and they forget that really God is the Father taking care of them and their families. They think it is all up to them—if they don't make the money, their families won't have all the things they need.

Little children are not like that. They don't worry about where their food and clothes will come from. They trust their mom and dad to give it to them. That is how children help grown-ups in the Church.

When it comes to getting to heaven, children just like you remind us we are all little children who can't do it ourselves. That is why our Father in heaven sent His Son, Jesus, to save us. Jesus lived on earth, carefully keeping all His Father's commands, and He died on the cross to pay for all the bad things we do. When He baptized us, God adopted us as His own children and opened heaven for us. We don't have to worry about food, clothes, a house, or anything that our families need— because God our Father promises He will take care of us.

Jesus' disciples stopped sending the parents and their children away. As they came near, they saw Jesus had a huge smile on His face as He spread His arms wide for the little children. He held them tight, put His hands on them, and blessed them.

As you grow up, don't forget how wonderful it feels to learn about God's love for you. You have a special place in Jesus' heart and a special place in His family. And before you grow up, please pray for God to help you remind your mom and dad, your grandparents, and all the grown-ups at church just how much they can trust Jesus.

LET'S PRAY: Lord Jesus, I am so happy that You care about little children like me. Give me Your Holy Spirit, so I can love Your Bible and always trust You like I trust You today. Amen.

Short Zacchaeus climbs a tree to see Jesus. Jesus calls him to come down so He can stay with him.

When was the last time you wanted to see something but were too short to see it?

Do you ever find it hard being young? When your feet don't reach the floor as you sit in a big chair? When you want to see an animal at the zoo, but can't see past the grown-ups standing in front of you?

Now imagine you are all grown up—but you are still small like you are today. You can't see when you are in a crowd of people. That's how it was for a tax collector named Zacchaeus (za-KEE-uhs). He lived in Jericho, and he learned that Jesus was passing through town on His way to the Passover in Jerusalem. Zacchaeus was a chief tax collector—in charge of all the tax collectors in the area. So the Jewish people hated him even more than they hated most tax collectors.

But Zacchaeus had heard things about Jesus. He heard Jesus talked to tax collectors and ate with them. Jesus even chose one named Matthew to be one of His twelve disciples. So when Zacchaeus heard Jesus was passing through town, he wanted to get a look at Him. But he was too short to see Jesus over the crowds. So he ran ahead and climbed up into a tree.

And sure enough, from the tree, Zacchaeus could see the big crowd of people coming through town. And in the middle of that crowd, he saw Jesus, coming closer and closer. Suddenly, Jesus came near his tree, stopped, and looked right up at him. With a big smile, Jesus said, "Zacchaeus, hurry and come down, for I must stay at your house today."

Zacchaeus was so happy that he rushed down, led Jesus to his house, and made a big feast for Him. As he talked with Jesus, he thought about the way he had treated the people he collected taxes from. He felt bad because he took more money than he should have.

He turned to Jesus and made a promise: "Behold, Lord, half of my goods I give to the poor. And if I have defrauded anyone of anything, I restore it fourfold." That meant if he took more money than he should have, he would pay back four times that amount.

Jesus replied, "Today salvation has come to this house, since he also is a son of Abraham. For I came to seek and to save the lost."

Imagine Jesus coming into your church. Everyone crowds around Him and you are trying to get a look, but you are too short to see. Suddenly, you hear Jesus telling everyone to step back because He has come to sit and talk with you. That's what He did when He baptized you. It is what He does every time you open this Bible and listen to His words. He sits beside you and talks with you. What a wonderful Savior we have!

LET'S PRAY: Lord Jesus, Zacchaeus was so happy when You told him to come down so You could go and spend the day with him. Thank You for coming to me in my Baptism and for talking to me when I read my Bible. Make me as excited as Zacchaeus to tell Your story to boys and girls who do not know You. Amen.

As Jesus rides into Jerusalem on a donkey, large crowds wave palm branches to welcome Him.

The Triumphal Entry

What is your favorite holiday? What makes it so special?

Every year in spring, the Jews gathered together in Jerusalem to celebrate the Passover feast. It was a time as happy and exciting for them as Christmas is for us. At Passover, the Jews remembered how God raised up Moses and used ten plagues to bring His people Israel out of slavery in Egypt. The people spread the blood of the Passover lamb on their doors, and when the angel saw the blood he passed over their houses, saving their firstborn.

Huge crowds came up the road to Jerusalem, and Jesus joined them just as He did many Passovers before. But this time, Jesus rode on a donkey. That's a work animal Jewish kings like King David rode into town. Roman kings and emperors rode on horses. The horse reminded the people of their king's power. But the donkey reminded the Jews that their King was coming to serve them, protect them, and take care of them.

The crowds around Jesus were very excited. They had traveled with Him, listened to His wonderful teachings, and seen the healing miracles He worked. They started singing and shouting many things to Jesus.

"Hosanna to the Son of David!" *Hosanna* means "save us now." They believed Jesus was the promised Savior, the Christ or Messiah. They asked Him to save them.

"Blessed is He who comes in the name of the Lord!" They said Jesus was happy to be coming on God's mission.

"Hosanna in the highest!" They shouted for God to save them through Jesus.

And they were right—that was exactly what Jesus was riding into Jerusalem to do for us. This Sunday started the most important week of all. On Sunday, Jesus rode into Jerusalem to save us from our sins. On Friday, He was punished on the cross for our sins, and He died in our place. Then on the following Sunday, He rose from the dead.

Sadly, many of the Jews traveling with Him did not yet understand this. They thought He had come to be an earthly king who would set Israel free and drive out the Romans. But Jesus came to save us from a bigger enemy than the Roman emperor. He came to save us from Satan and being separated forever from God in hell.

Next time you go to church and there is Communion, notice the song we sing when we get ready for Communion. We sing many of the same words these crowds were singing and shouting to Jesus. The reason we do this is because we are celebrating that Jesus is coming to us again—to give us His body and blood with the bread and wine of Communion. In a few years, you will be receiving His body and blood for yourself. But as you wait for that great day, be sure to sing this song with joy because Jesus is coming.

LET'S PRAY: Lord Jesus, it was a great day when You rode the donkey into Jerusalem. You came to save us from our sins. Thank You for coming to us in so many ways now—in Baptism, in Your Bible, and in Holy Communion. Amen.

77

Jesus is angry to see animals being sold right in the temple. He makes a whip and drives them out.

Jesus Clears the Temple

Can you think of a time when it would be okay to be angry with someone?

Jesus rode a donkey into Jerusalem on the Sunday before He died on the cross. Large crowds of people welcomed Him; they shouted and sang. But not everyone was happy to see Jesus ride into Jerusalem. The chief priests and Jewish leaders didn't believe in Jesus, and it made them really mad to hear people singing and shouting to Him that He was the great Savior God had promised to Adam and Eve. These leaders wanted to find a way to get rid of Jesus, but they were afraid the crowds would turn against them.

Jesus went up to the temple grounds to teach. When He entered the temple, He got really, really angry. He saw tables set up for people to buy animals they needed for their sacrifices. There were birdcages with pigeons and doves. There were sheep and lambs, goats and bulls. The animals were noisy, and the people buying and selling them had to shout to be heard over that noise.

Jesus knew people needed to buy animals for their sacrifices, so that wasn't what made Him mad. He was upset that they were doing this in the temple! These should have been sold in the market a short way across town. People came to the temple to worship God, hear His Word, and pray. But how could they hear and pray when there was so much noise from the animals, the people shouting, and the coins clinking on the tables?

Jesus suddenly ran up to the tables and flipped them upside down. The coins went flying everywhere! He knocked over the chairs the people were sitting on to sell the birds. He made a whip out of cords and drove away the animals and the people who were buying and selling (John 2:15). He told them, "It is written,

'My house will be called a house of prayer,' but you have made it a den of robbers.'"

Worship and prayer are very important to Jesus. They should be important to you and me too. God comes to us when we pray and read His Word, when we sing together in church. That is why our parents tell us to be quiet in church—so that we will pay attention to what God is saying to us, and so the people sitting around us will be able to listen to the pastor teach and preach.

That is also why we fold our hands, close our eyes, and bow our heads when we pray. Hands that are folded together won't reach for things that will take our attention away from God. Eyes that are closed won't be looking for things to think about instead of what is being prayed. Heads that are bowed make it a little harder to hear strange noises and voices that make us try to figure out where they are coming from.

This is what being in God's house is all about, why we listen and pray—so God can come to us, speak to us, and remind us just how much He loves us.

LET'S PRAY: Lord Jesus, thank You for clearing out the temple court so the people You love could hear what You wanted to tell them. Clear my mind when I read Your Bible, when I pray, and when I am in church and Sunday School, so I can listen to Your wonderful promises. Amen.

At Jesus' last meal before He died, He washes all His disciples' feet to show how He loves them.

The Lord's Supper

Matthew 26:17–35

What do you think it would have been like to eat supper with Jesus?

On Friday, Jesus would die on the cross. But on Thursday night, He gathered with His twelve disciples for one last meal together—the Passover. He wanted to show them how much He loved them, and He wanted to make them ready for the terrible things they would soon see.

But first, Jesus got up from the table and took off His outer clothes (like we would take off a jacket). He wrapped a towel around His waist, got down on His hands and knees, and washed His disciples' feet. He taught us that no job is too low or dirty when we can show people how much we love them. When He was done, He sat back down and they started eating (see John 13:1–11).

Then Jesus felt really sad and upset. He knew one of His twelve disciples did not love Him like before and was planning to do something bad. Jesus knew Judas had been paid money from the Jewish leaders who hated Jesus. Judas promised to tell them when they could arrest Jesus without the big crowds around. Jesus loved Judas as a brother—but Judas was treating Him like an enemy.

Jesus told the twelve disciples, "One of you will betray Me." The disciples were upset. Looking at one another, each one asked Jesus, "Is it I?" Jesus answered, "It is he to whom I will give this morsel of bread when I have dipped it" (John 13:26). He dipped it in a bowl and then gave it to Judas and said, "What you are going to do, do quickly" (John 13:27). Right away, Judas went out into the darkness of night. None of the other disciples realized what Judas was going to do.

Later, Jesus took some bread, said a prayer of thanks for it, broke it, and gave it to His disciples. He said, "Take, eat; this is My body." Then after supper, Jesus took a cup of wine. He said a prayer of thanks, then gave it to His disciples and said, "Drink of it, all of you, for this is My blood of the covenant, which is poured out for many for the forgiveness of sins."

Then Jesus told His disciples that during that same night all of them would run away from Him. Peter answered, "Though they all fall away because of You, I will never fall away." Jesus told him, "Truly, I tell you, this very night, before the rooster crows, you will deny Me three times." Peter said, "Even if I must die with You, I will not deny You!"

Can you imagine what it would have been like to be in that Upper Room and have Jesus get down on His hands and knees to wash your feet? When you were baptized, Jesus did something like that. He was right there with you, washing away all of your sins. When you get older, you will be able to receive Holy Communion. Jesus will come to you again in the bread and wine, giving you His very own body and blood, which took away your sins on the cross.

LET'S PRAY: Lord Jesus, You loved me and washed away all my sins. Help me show my love to my family and my friends, too, and tell them about Your love. Amen.

Before Jesus is ready to die on the cross, He prays to His Father, telling Him all His feelings.

Jesus Prays in the Garden

Tell about a time you had to do something you really didn't want to do.

After the Last Supper, Jesus led His disciples up the Mount of Olives to a place called the Garden of Gethsemane (geth-SEM-uh-nee). Leaving eight disciples behind, He took Peter, James, and John along with Him. He told them to watch with Him and pray, and then He walked on about as far as you can throw a stone. Then He knelt down and prayed.

Doesn't it seem like praying should be really easy? There in the garden, Jesus showed us it can be very, very hard sometimes. He loved His Father, and He wanted to do what His Father sent Him to do. He wanted to save us, but it hurt Him to think about what would happen on that cross. It wasn't just that the nails would really, really hurt. It wasn't just that His friends would all leave Him and He would be surrounded by people making fun of Him. What really hurt was knowing God His Father would turn against Him and punish Him for all our sins.

Jesus was crying when He prayed, "Father, if You are willing, remove this cup from Me. Nevertheless, not My will, but Yours, be done." No matter what, Jesus wanted to do what His heavenly Father wanted, and He wanted to save us from our sins. But He asked if there was any other way than the cross. Knowing there wasn't, He prayed, "Not My will, but Yours, be done."

God the Father saw how much His Son was hurting. So He sent an angel to strengthen Jesus. After that, Jesus prayed even harder. He prayed so hard He was sweating, and blood mixed in with that sweat.

Jesus prayed for nearly an hour; then, He went to check on Peter, James, and John. They were all sleeping. Jesus woke them up and reminded them to pray.

Jesus went away and started praying again.

He said the same thing this second time: "My Father, if this cannot pass unless I drink it, Your will be done" (Matthew 26:42). After another hour of praying, Jesus checked in on the three disciples again. But they were still sleeping.

One more time, Jesus returned to pray. After another hour, praying the same words again, Jesus was finally ready to go to the cross and save us from sin and hell.

He woke up His disciples and told them it was time to go; Judas was coming.

Sometimes, praying is a very, very hard thing to do, like when we have to face a bully, take a test, give a report, go to a doctor or the dentist, have surgery, or move away from all our friends. These are the times it is hard to pray Jesus' words "Not what I want, but what You want, God!"

But Jesus promises to be right there with you when you pray. And at the end, that problem will pass away, just as Jesus' hours on the cross finally came to an end.

LET'S PRAY: Lord Jesus, thank You for praying so You were ready to go to the cross for all of us. Give me courage and strength to pray in hard times so I'll be ready to do what You want too! Amen.

One of Jesus' disciples named Judas leads a crowd to grab Him and take Him to the priests.

What would you do if someone did something really, really mean to you?

After the Last Supper, Jesus went out to pray in the Garden of Gethsemane. When He was finished, He woke up His disciples and watched a crowd coming toward the garden. They were carrying torches, clubs, and swords. In front was one of the Twelve—Judas.

After all that time praying, Jesus was ready. He stepped forward, past the other disciples, to meet Judas and the soldiers as they came near.

Judas walked up to Jesus and kissed Him so the crowd would know whom to arrest. Jesus asked, "Judas, would you betray the Son of Man with a kiss?" (Luke 22:48).

Judas didn't realize what a terrible thing he was doing—but Jesus knew that later, when Judas saw that Jesus would be put to death on the cross, he would feel really, really guilty. If only Judas would remember how much Jesus loved him. If only he would wait until the third day when Jesus rose from the dead! Then, Jesus could have appeared to him, forgiven him, and given him back his place among the Twelve.

Jesus turned from Judas to the soldiers and asked whom they were looking for. They answered, "Jesus of Nazareth." With the powerful voice of the Son of God, Jesus answered, "I am He." His words were so powerful they pushed the crowd backward and made them fall to the ground. Judas fell down with them.

When they got back up, Jesus again asked whom they were looking for. For a second time, they answered, "Jesus of Nazareth." Jesus said, "I told you that I am He. So, if you seek Me, let these men go." And with that, Jesus let His eleven disciples run away to safety. But Peter didn't realize Jesus was in control. He grabbed a sword, ran up to the soldiers, and swung it down with all his might. It cut off the ear of the high priest's servant.

Before the soldiers could strike back, Jesus stepped forward, turned to Peter and said, "Put your sword away. Shall I not drink the cup that the Father has given Me?" He walked to the wounded man, touched his ear, and healed him (see Luke 22:51). The eleven disciples scattered, and the guards and soldiers tied Jesus up and led Him back into Jerusalem.

As Jesus found with Judas, it hurts really, really badly when someone you love, someone you trust, does something bad to you. We want to be angry with that person forever, to never, ever be his or her friend again. But Jesus warns us not to hold onto that kind of anger. It may feel good for a little while, but God wants us to keep loving and forgiving others the way Jesus kept loving Judas and keeps loving and forgiving each of us.

LET'S PRAY: Jesus, it hurt You really badly when Judas betrayed You. But You still loved him and wanted to forgive him. Teach me how to stay away from sins like Judas's, but when I do sin, help me realize what I have done and turn to You to ask Your forgiveness. Then, I can live in peace and joy as I tell others about Your wonderful love. Amen.

The Jewish leaders hold a trial to kill Jesus. Their leader is the high priest named Caiaphas.

How does it feel to be blamed for doing something you didn't do?

Jesus left the Last Supper and then went to pray. There in the garden, He was arrested, and the guards and soldiers led Him to the house of the high priest Caiaphas (KAY-uh-fuhs). All the Jewish judges were gathered for Jesus' trial. In a trial, a person is accused of doing something bad. Judges listen to witnesses who saw or heard what happened, and then they decide if the person did it or not.

So Jesus was on trial, but it wasn't going to be a fair trial. Jesus hadn't done anything wrong, but the judges wanted to put Him to death anyway. They were angry because Jesus said things that showed the people they were sinners who needed forgiveness. They were also afraid the crowds would make Him a king and the Romans would come in and destroy the temple.

But as Caiaphas the high priest started the trial, he was having a hard time. Way back in Moses' time, God gave Israel a rule that said two witnesses had to agree before someone could be punished for doing something wrong—one witness was not enough. And the high priest couldn't find two witnesses who said the same thing. Even when the high priest looked for witnesses to lie about Jesus, he still couldn't find two stories that matched.

The high priest finally turned to Jesus. He said, "Tell us if You are the Christ, the Son of God." Jesus answered, "You have said so." He meant everything the high priest said was true—Jesus was and is the Christ, the Son of God. But Jesus didn't stop there. He warned the Jewish leaders that they would all see Him sitting at God the Father's right hand and coming on the clouds of heaven to be their judge on Judgment Day.

That was what the high priest was hoping to hear. Now he could accuse Jesus of claiming to be God—which would be a terrible thing for Jesus to say if it were not true. But it was true and always will be true. The high priest asked the Jewish court what they had decided. They said Jesus should die on the cross for saying He was God's Son.

Even though they wanted Jesus to die, they couldn't put Jesus to death on the cross. Only Pontius Pilate (PON-shuhs PIGH-luht), the Roman governor, could do that. But it was the middle of the night, and they had to wait until the sun came up to take Jesus to Pilate. So the leaders took turns hitting Jesus, slapping Him in the face, and spitting on Him. They covered His eyes with a blindfold and then hit Him in the face and demanded that He tell them who had struck Him.

Jesus stood silently and let Himself get beaten up. Why? Because that is what you and I and all of us deserve for all the bad things we do to one another—and for not doing the good things we should do. In this trial, we see Jesus already carrying our sins and suffering in our place so we will never have to.

LET'S PRAY: Jesus, You were hurt by the people You loved and were ready to go to the cross to save. Forgive me for the times I don't do what You say and treat other people badly. Amen.

While Jesus is being tried, His disciple Peter is so scared he says he doesn't know Jesus.

Peter Denies Jesus

Mark 14:53–54, 66–72

Have you ever had the chance to speak up for someone who was being treated badly, but you kept quiet? What kept you from helping that person?

After Jesus was arrested in the garden, He was taken to the high priest's house. While He was inside being questioned, Peter was sitting with the guards in the high priest's courtyard. He wanted to find out what was happening to Jesus. At first, he seemed very brave to be there, but soon Peter wished he had run away like the other disciples.

It all started when a servant girl walked up to Peter and said, "You also were with the Nazarene, Jesus."

Peter was scared of the guards and soldiers and what they would do to him, so he said, "I neither know nor understand what you mean." That was Peter's first denial.

Peter was scared to stay there with the guards, so he walked toward the gateway. As he did, a rooster crowed.

But the servant girl again told the bystanders, "This man is one of them."

He lied and for the second time denied knowing Jesus.

The guards were quiet for a little bit, but before long they gathered around him again. They had listened carefully to what Peter had said—and how he had said it. They noticed Peter didn't talk like they did; he was from the north, and they were from the south.

They said, "Certainly you, too, are one of them, for you are a Galilean."

Peter knew he was in big trouble; no one was believing him. So he swore, which means he asked God to listen to what he said and punish him if he was lying. And he called down a curse on himself, something like, "If I know this Jesus, may God strike me dead!"

Clearly Peter wasn't thinking about God—he was just looking for some way to save himself from the guards and what they might do to him. He should have thought about what Jesus once taught him: "Do not fear those who kill the body but cannot kill the soul. Rather fear Him who can destroy both soul and body in hell" (Matthew 10:28).

But Peter wasn't thinking about Judgment Day, or of how God could punish him in hell. All he could think of was how to get out of there alive. He said, "I do not know this man of whom you speak."

And while he was still saying his third denial, Peter heard the rooster crow again. He remembered how Jesus had told him at the Last Supper, "Before the rooster crows twice, you will deny Me three times." Then Peter went outside the courtyard and started crying very hard.

As Peter learned, it is hard to speak up for a person when everyone else in the crowd is attacking that person. But that is exactly what Jesus did when He was dying on the cross. He prayed, "Father, forgive them, for they know not what they do" (Luke 23:34). Now, He gives you courage and strength to share the Good News of His death and resurrection.

LET'S PRAY: Lord Jesus, You felt the sting of Peter's denials. Forgive me the times I stay quiet when You want me to speak up. Give me courage to tell everyone I meet about Your love. Amen.

The Jews bring Jesus to Pilate, the Roman governor. Pilate orders Jesus to hang on a cross.

Jesus before Pontius Pilate

What would you do if a bunch of kids wanted you to do something that was wrong?

After He was arrested, Jesus was led to the Jewish leaders, who decided He must die. But the Romans would not let them put a person to death. Only the Roman governor, Pontius Pilate (PON-shuhs PIGH-luht), could do that. Early Friday morning, they brought Jesus before him.

Pilate asked what Jesus had done wrong.

The Jewish leaders told Pilate that Jesus had broken three laws: "We found this man misleading our nation and forbidding us to give tribute to Caesar, and saying that He Himself is Christ, a king" (Luke 23:2). Pilate went into his headquarters and asked Jesus, "Are You the King of the Jews?"

Jesus answered, "My kingdom is not of this world. If My kingdom were of this world, My servants would have been fighting, that I might not be delivered over to the Jews. But My kingdom is not from the world."

Pilate answered, "So You are a king?"

Jesus answered, "You say that I am a king. I have come into the world to bear witness to the truth. Everyone who is of the truth listens to My voice."

Pilate told the Jews, "I find no guilt in Him." But instead of setting Jesus free, he thought he could make the Jews ask him to set Jesus free. He said, "You have a custom that I should release one man for you at the Passover." He asked them to choose between Jesus and Barabbas (buh-RAB-uhs), a really bad man who had killed some people. The Jewish leaders convinced the crowds to call for Barabbas to be set free and for Jesus to be crucified.

Pilate was surprised. He knew Jesus had done nothing wrong, but he thought if he had Jesus whipped that would satisfy the leaders who hated Jesus so much.

So the Roman soldiers took Jesus and whipped Him really badly. They made a crown out of thorns and put it on His head. They put a purple robe on Him and kneeled in front of Him, saying, "Hail, King of the Jews!"

Pilate brought Jesus out to the Jews and said, "Behold the man!" He hoped the Jews would think Jesus had already suffered enough. But when they saw Him, they shouted, "Crucify Him, crucify Him!"

Finally, Pilate gave up. He took a bowl and washed his hands in front of them all, and said, "I am innocent of this man's blood" (Matthew 27:24). He set Barabbas free and ordered his soldiers to take Jesus outside the city and crucify Him.

When people bigger or more powerful than us threaten us because of our faith in Jesus, we know what we should say, but we are afraid. We are afraid of what people will think or say or do to us if we speak of Jesus being our hope and Savior. The Holy Spirit promises to be with us to make us bold and strong so we can speak of Jesus when no one else will. When we fail, we can tell God we are sorry and know that Jesus suffered and died to take away all our sin and that the Holy Spirit empowers us.

LET'S PRAY: Lord Jesus, You told Pilate about the kingdom of heaven because You wanted him to believe and be saved. Give me and all Christians courage to speak up for You and to defend one another so the world will know You love them too. Amen.

91

Jesus is nailed to a cross. He hurts and dies to take away the punishment for all of our sins.

The Crucifixion and Jesus' Last Words

Why did Jesus die on the cross?

The Roman soldiers made Jesus carry His cross through Jerusalem to a hill called Golgotha outside the city. There, they nailed His hands and feet to the cross and raised Him up between two criminals (see Mark 15:27). They put a sign over His head that read, "Jesus of Nazareth, the King of the Jews."

Jesus prayed, "Father, forgive them, for they know not what they do" (Luke 23:34). He was praying for the Roman soldiers, but also for Judas and Peter, Caiaphas the high priest and the Jewish court, Pontius Pilate, the criminals who were making fun of Him, the crowds who were watching, and for you, me, and all people, because He was being punished for all our sins.

At first, both criminals made fun of Jesus (see Matthew 27:44). But then, one changed his mind. He asked the other, "Do you not fear God?" (Luke 23:40). He knew he would stand before God to be judged after he died. He told the other they both had done very bad things and deserved to die on a cross. But Jesus had done nothing wrong. In the faith given to him by the Holy Spirit, he prayed, "Jesus, remember me when You come into Your kingdom" (v. 42). Jesus said, "Truly, I say to you, today you will be with Me in paradise" (v. 43).

Jesus looked out and saw His mother, Mary, and His friend John, one of the twelve disciples. Jesus looked at Mary, nodded His head toward John, and said, "Woman, behold your son!" Then, He looked at John, nodded toward Mary, and said, "Behold, your mother!" From that hour, John took Mary into his home and took care of her.

At noon, the sun stopped shining and it grew very dark (see Luke 23:44). Jesus was being punished in our place for our sins. God the Father left Jesus all alone to suffer the punishment for all our sins. This went on for three long hours until Jesus cried out, "My God, My God, why have You forsaken Me?" (Matthew 27:46).

When Jesus knew all our sins were paid in full, He said, "I thirst." The soldiers gave Him some sour wine to drink.

After drinking, Jesus shouted in a loud voice, "It is finished." He had finished everything God the Father had sent Him to do. The serpent's head was crushed (see Genesis 3:15). Every sin had been paid for, and heaven now stood open for everyone who believes in Jesus.

Finally, Jesus prayed, "Father, into Your hands I commit My spirit" (Luke 23:46). Then, He died.

Many people are scared to die. But we don't have to be. Jesus went there first. He died, was buried, and rose to life again. Like He promised the criminal who died next to Him, He promises all who believe in Him that when we die, our spirits will leave this world of hurts and sorrows and be with Him in paradise. Then, on the Last Day, He will come back and raise our bodies to everlasting life.

LET'S PRAY: Lord Jesus, whenever I am afraid of dying, remind me of Your death and resurrection. Remind me You will take my spirit home to heaven when I die and raise my body back to life when You come back. Amen.

93

Two men lay Jesus' dead body in a tomb while women who loved Jesus watch.

Jesus Is Buried

Why is it sad when someone dies?

Jesus died on the cross at about 3:00 in the afternoon. The sad women stood by the cross wondering what would happen to His body. They saw two Jewish leaders come up to the crosses. Both were from the Jewish court that decided Jesus should die. But these two did not agree with that decision. They were followers of Jesus who kept their faith secret—until now.

One was Nicodemus, a Jewish leader who once visited Jesus at night (John 3). He believed Jesus was from God and even told the Jewish leaders they should give Jesus a fair chance (John 7:50–51). The second was a man named Joseph from a town called Arimathea (air-ih-muh-THEE-uh). He was a very important Jewish leader. He was a good man who was looking for the promised Savior and believed Jesus was that Savior. But he didn't tell anyone because he was afraid the other Jewish leaders would throw him out of the Jewish court.

After Jesus died, Joseph went to Pontius Pilate and asked him for permission to take Jesus' body down from the cross and bury it. When Pilate learned Jesus was dead, he gave Joseph permission.

Joseph and Nicodemus took Jesus' body down from the cross. It was late, and they had to hurry before the sun went down and the day of rest started. While they carried Jesus' body to Joseph's own new tomb in a garden nearby, the women followed them.

Joseph and Nicodemus cleaned Jesus' body as best they could and wrapped it in cloth with spices. They laid it in the tomb and then rolled a huge stone over the entrance and walked away. The women paid close attention so they could remember where the tomb was. They went home and planned to buy more spices so when Sunday morning came, they could return and give Jesus' body a more careful, loving burial.

Meanwhile on Saturday morning, the chief priests remembered something Jesus said before He died. He said He would be killed and rise again on the third day. They really didn't believe Jesus would come alive again—they didn't believe there was life after someone died. But they were afraid Jesus' disciples might steal His body from the tomb and start telling people He rose from the dead.

So they went to Pilate and asked for soldiers to guard Jesus' tomb to make sure this wouldn't happen. Pilate gave them soldiers who went and stood watch at the tomb to make sure Jesus' body stayed there.

When we die, our spirits will go to be with Jesus in paradise, just like the robber who died with Him (Luke 23:39–43). We will see Him shining in glory, and we will be very happy and excited. We won't really worry about what will happen to our bodies—God will take care of them. On the Last Day, Jesus will return and raise our bodies to life again.

LET'S PRAY: Lord God, heavenly Father, thank You for sending Joseph and Nicodemus to take care of Jesus' body. Remind us that You will take care of us all through life—and even after we die—until Jesus returns and raises our bodies and makes them perfect and shining in bright glory forever. In Jesus' name. Amen.

A mighty angel rolls the stone away from Jesus' tomb. The frightened guards fall on the ground.

Jesus Rises from the Dead

Matthew 28:1–10

Think of a time when you were really, really sad. Did you ever think you could be happy again?

Many times during the months before Jesus went up to Jerusalem, He told His disciples He was going to suffer and die. And each time, He also told them He would rise again on the third day. But the disciples didn't remember. They all thought He was going to Jerusalem to become king—instead, they saw Him killed on the cross. Their dreams of ruling with Jesus were dead, and they were filled with sadness. They forgot all about His promise to rise again.

On the second day, Saturday, they stayed hidden in Jerusalem because they were afraid they would be captured and killed too. Since that day was a Sabbath, the women rested, waiting for the third day, Sunday, to take spices and give Jesus' body a better burial. They forgot all about His promise to rise from the dead too.

Early Sunday morning, the women started off for the tomb. As they walked along, they remembered the huge stone Joseph and Nicodemus had rolled in front of it. They weren't strong enough to roll it back, so they wondered how they were going to get inside.

Suddenly there was an earthquake, and an angel came down from heaven, rolled the stone back, and sat on it. When the guards saw the angel, they were terrified. They shook and fell down like they were dead. The angel waited for the women.

When the women came, the angel told them, "Do not be afraid, for I know that you are looking for Jesus who was crucified. He is not here, for He has risen, as He said. Come, see the place where He lay."

They looked in and saw that Jesus' body was missing. There was only the cloth and some spices lying where His body had been.

The angel told them, "Go quickly and tell His disciples that He has risen from the dead, and behold, He is going before you to Galilee; there you will see Him."

The women turned and rushed back toward the city to tell Jesus' disciples. But while they were on the way, Jesus met them and said, "Greetings!" They came close, grabbed hold of His feet, and worshiped Him. Jesus told them, "Do not be afraid; go and tell My brothers to go to Galilee, and there they will see Me."

Friday had been the saddest day in these women's lives, but on Sunday morning Jesus turned their sorrow into great joy. Sometimes we have sad days when bad things happen and they leave us hurt. We might think we will never be happy again. But Jesus can take away that hurt. By His death and resurrection, He has given us a bright, new future. Like the women, we have a very good reason to rejoice and be happy!

LET'S PRAY: Lord Jesus, God Your Father raised You from the dead to show You took away our sins and destroyed them on the cross. When bad things happen and I'm scared and sad, fill me with joy and peace, because You are with me to take care of me and lead me to my home in heaven. Amen.

Jesus walks and talks with two of His followers during the afternoon after He rose from the dead.

On the Road to Emmaus

Luke 24:13–35

Did you ever hear news so good you felt you were burning inside?

Jesus died on the cross on Friday; He rose from the dead on Sunday. Some of the women went out to the tomb and heard the angels' good news that Jesus had risen; then they saw Jesus and talked with Him.

When the women told the disciples that they had talked with Jesus, the men didn't believe them. Two men were so sad and upset, they left Jerusalem. These two were not part of Jesus' twelve apostles. They were part of a larger group of disciples or believers. One was named Cleopas (KLEE-oh-puhs), but we don't know the name of the other.

They walked along a road that passed through a village called Emmaus (ih-MAY-us). As they walked along, they talked about all the things that had happened. Jesus came near and started walking along with them, but they didn't recognize Him. He asked them, "What are you talking about?"

They stopped walking and looked at Him with sad faces. Cleopas asked Him, "Are You the only visitor to Jerusalem who does not know the things that have happened there?" Jesus answered, "What things?"

The two started telling Jesus about Himself. They said He was a prophet who was mighty in what He said and did. They told how the chief priests and rulers had handed Him over to Pilate and that He had been crucified. They talked about how they had thought Jesus was going to save Israel.

Then they said, "Some women from our company amazed us. They were at the tomb early this morning, and when they didn't find His body, they came back saying they had seen angels who said He was alive."

Jesus said, "O foolish ones, and slow of heart to believe all that the prophets have spoken!"

He told them the Messiah had to suffer like this first and then enter His glory by rising from the dead. Then He went through the Old Testament and taught them what God had written about His suffering, death, and resurrection.

By now it was late in the day. The two disciples were stopping in Emmaus for the night, but Jesus acted like He was going to go farther. The two begged Him to stay with them, so He went inside. They sat down for supper, and Jesus took the bread, broke it, said a prayer of thanks, and handed it to them. Suddenly they recognized Jesus—and then He vanished from their sight.

They talked about the wonderful burning feeling they had felt inside when Jesus was walking and talking with them. They were so excited that they ran back to Jerusalem, found Jesus' disciples, and told them how Jesus had walked and talked with them along the road.

Our lives on earth can't always be happy. Bad things happen to us and to the people we love, and those things make us sad. But we don't have to be sad forever. Jesus rose from the dead, and He walks with us every day of our lives. Jesus gives us a joy that no sadness can take away forever.

LET'S PRAY: Heavenly Father, since Jesus died on the cross for my sins, I never have to be afraid You will stop loving me. And because He rose from the dead, I know I will rise again too—and then everything will be perfect forever and ever. Show me someone who needs to hear about Jesus, and give me courage to speak. In Jesus' name. Amen.

Jesus shows Himself to His followers in a locked room in Jerusalem the night after He rose.

Jesus Appears to His Apostles

Think of something really neat that happened at school or with your friends. Now, try to describe it to people from your family who weren't there to see it.

It was the Sunday Jesus rose from the dead. Late in the afternoon, the two men who met Jesus on the road to Emmaus rushed back to Jerusalem. They told the disciples how they had walked and talked with Jesus. The disciples told them that Jesus had appeared to Peter all by himself earlier that afternoon.

While the men were talking about all this exciting news, suddenly Jesus was standing among them, saying, "Peace to you!" Everyone was shocked and scared—they thought they were looking at a ghost because Jesus suddenly appeared, and the door of the house was locked. He asked why they doubted it was really Him. "See My hands and My feet. Touch Me, and see. For a spirit does not have flesh and bones as you see that I have."

There in His hands, they could see the marks from the nails that had held Him to the cross, and they saw the same in His feet. Their shock and fear turned to wonder and amazement. But Jesus wanted them to be sure, so He asked if they had any food left to eat. They gave Him a piece of fish they had broiled, and He ate it in front of them. Now they knew for sure He was not a ghost.

Jesus began to teach them why He had to die on the cross and rise again on the third day. He went through the Old Testament in the Bible and showed them places where God's prophets had told His people bits and pieces of what the Messiah would do when He came to save the world. He opened their minds so they could understand the Old Testament and believe that He was the Messiah who had to "suffer and on the third day rise from the dead."

Jesus told them their work would soon begin. Since they had seen everything Jesus did, God would send them power from on high, from heaven, and they would start teaching the Jews, the Samaritans, and all the people in the world that we must be sorry for our sins and receive the forgiveness Jesus won when He died for those sins on the cross.

None of us was there to see all that Jesus did to save us from our sins. But the Bible tells us the things Jesus said and did in front of His twelve apostles and many other men and women who saw and heard Him. When we read the Bible, Jesus opens our minds so we can see and hear the same things those people did. Then we are ready to go and tell our friends and neighbors how Jesus came to save us from our sins by dying on the cross and rising to life again on the third day.

LET'S PRAY: Lord Jesus, thank You for coming to earth to suffer and die and save us all from our sins. Thank You also for rising again on the third day—that makes us all so happy. Now, make me bold and fill me with joy so I share this Good News every chance I can. Amen.

Thomas did not believe Jesus rose. A week later, Jesus appears and shows Himself to Thomas.

Jesus Appears to Thomas

Do you know someone who thinks she knows everything—but she really doesn't?

On the evening of that first Sunday when Jesus rose from the dead, He appeared to His disciples, who were hiding behind locked doors. But Thomas, one of the twelve disciples Jesus chose, wasn't there that night. Later on, when Thomas joined them again, Peter and the other disciples told him over and over again, "We have seen the Lord."

But Thomas thought they were being foolish. He would not let himself believe Jesus was alive unless he saw Him for himself. And even more than that, Thomas insisted that he would have to do more than just look at Jesus to believe He was really alive. He said, "Unless I see in His hands the mark of the nails, and place my finger into the mark of the nails, and place my hand into His side, I will never believe."

Thomas thought the other disciples were foolish, but really he was the one who was being stubborn and silly. He had seen Jesus heal blind, deaf, and paralyzed people; he had seen Jesus walk on water and make storms stop instantly; he had even seen Jesus raise Lazarus from the dead—so why did he refuse to believe Jesus could have risen from the dead?

Jesus could have left Thomas alone in his sad unbelief, but one week later, on the next Sunday night, Jesus made a special visit to the disciples. This time, Thomas was with them. Even though the door was locked, Jesus came and stood among them. He said, "Peace be with you." Then, He turned to Thomas, held out His hands, and said, "Put your finger here, and see My hands; and put out your hand, and place it in My side." He told Thomas to stop refusing to believe, and believe.

Thomas answered, "My Lord and my God!"

Jesus answered, "Have you believed because you have seen Me? Blessed are those who have not seen and yet have believed."

Plenty of people are like Thomas. They refuse to believe anything they can't see and touch. They think we are foolish to believe that God created the world or that He sent a terrible flood from which only Noah's family survived or that Jesus rose from the dead. They think they are smarter than that! That's what Thomas thought—until Jesus appeared to him.

God is so much bigger, stronger, and smarter than any of us will ever be. If He tells us something in His Bible, we can believe it and we should believe it—no matter what people in our world think and no matter how smart they seem to be. People may say you have to be really stupid to believe in Jesus, but remember this: That is how Thomas once felt. He didn't feel that way after he saw Jesus! And like the other disciples, Thomas was so sure Jesus died and rose again that he was willing to die rather than say it wasn't true.

LET'S PRAY: Lord Jesus, thank You for showing Yourself to Thomas so he could stop being so stubborn and know that You are really alive again. Help me trust everything You say. Amen.

After breakfast by the Sea of Galilee, Jesus talks with Peter to let him know He still loves him.

Jesus Restores Peter

John 21:1–19

Have you ever really hurt a friend and felt so guilty that you were afraid to see him again? What could you do to be sure he still loves you?

A few weeks after Jesus rose from the dead, Peter and Jesus' other disciples went back to Galilee. Peter told them, "I am going fishing." Several disciples joined him. They spent all that night fishing but didn't catch even one fish.

Early in the morning, a man on the shore called out to them, "Children, do you have any fish?" They answered no. He said, "Cast the net on the right side of the boat, and you will find some." They did—and the net was so heavy with fish they were not able to haul it into the boat.

Right away, John told Peter, "It is the Lord!" Simon Peter immediately threw himself into the water and swam to shore. The others rowed the boat in because they were not far from shore. When Peter came close to Jesus, he saw a charcoal fire with fish cooking on it. When the disciples arrived, they ate the breakfast Jesus had prepared for them.

After breakfast, Jesus turned to Peter and asked, "Simon, son of John, do you love Me more than these?" Peter was quick to answer, "Yes, Lord; You know that I love You." Jesus told him, "Feed My lambs."

A second time, Jesus asked, "Simon, son of John, do you love Me?" Peter answered, "Yes, Lord; You know that I love You." Jesus answered, "Tend My sheep."

Then, a third time, Jesus asked Peter, "Simon, son of John, do you love Me?" Peter was hurt. Didn't Jesus believe him?

Jesus was making Peter think about the Last Supper, when Jesus had told Peter he would deny Him three times before the rooster crowed. Peter had argued that he would never deny knowing Jesus. But a few hours later, he had denied Him three times as he stood outside with the guards warming himself by the charcoal fire. Three times, Peter had had the chance to show how much he loved Jesus, but each time he had said, "I don't know the man."

Peter could not prove his love—not here by the Sea of Galilee. He didn't try to argue like he did at the Last Supper. All he could do was ask Jesus to look into his heart. He said, "Lord, You know everything; You know that I love You." Jesus answered, "Feed My sheep."

Then, He told Peter what would happen many years later. He told Peter he would get the chance to show his love for Jesus again—and this time the Holy Spirit would make Peter strong to die on a cross, showing his great love for Jesus.

Sometimes, we do bad things that make us feel so awful, like we could never be loved again. But just as Jesus forgave Peter and made him strong to do the work God wanted him to do, Jesus forgives us and makes us strong to love one another and serve God.

LET'S PRAY: Lord Jesus, thank You for making Peter strong again. Make me strong when I am weak, so I can tell others of Your love. Amen.

Forty days after Jesus rose from the dead, He lifts off the ground and rises up to heaven.

Jesus Ascends into Heaven

Luke 24:50–53

Do you have grandparents or family members who live far away? How does it feel when they have to leave after a visit?

For forty days after He rose from the dead, Jesus showed Himself to His disciples in many different places and times. There was no doubt that He had died but was alive again.

One of the last times He showed Himself was on a mountain in Galilee. A large number of disciples were gathered there, and Jesus told them, "All authority in heaven and on earth has been given to Me." That means Jesus controls everything that happens on this earth—even when it looks like the devil is in control.

Jesus went on: "Go therefore and make disciples of all nations, baptizing them in the name of the Father and of the Son and of the Holy Spirit, teaching them to observe all that I have commanded you." This is the great mission Jesus gave to us, His Church. We are to tell the world, our neighbors, our family, and our friends about His great love—how He took our sins upon Himself and suffered and died on the cross in our place. We are to tell them He rose from the dead on the third day to destroy the power of death.

If that sounds like a hard thing to do, don't worry. Jesus added a great promise: "And behold, I am with you always, to the end of the age" (Matthew 28:20). Wherever we go, whatever we do, Jesus will always be there to help us, keep us safe in faith, and give us everything we need.

Finally, forty days after He rose from the dead, Jesus gathered His disciples in Jerusalem again. He told them they would be His witnesses. They would tell people about His life, His words, and His mighty miracles. They would tell about His suffering and death on the cross that took away all their sins, and about His powerful resurrection on Easter that gave them eternal life.

Jesus walked with them to Bethany. Then, while He was talking with them, He suddenly started to rise up off the ground. While they watched, He rose higher and higher into the air until He went up through the clouds and left them. He entered heaven and sat down at the right hand of God His Father. Now, He prays for us and rules everything that happens in the whole world for the good of His Church. He will be at the Father's right hand until Judgment Day comes. Then, He will come back down from heaven with all His angels to judge the world.

If you have grandparents or an aunt or uncle who lives far away, you know how sad it can be when they have to leave you or you have to leave them after a visit. It might seem sad that Jesus rose up—ascended—into heaven, but that doesn't mean He left us. Jesus is always here with us, living in our hearts, speaking to us through the Bible, forgiving our sins, and protecting and guiding us.

LET'S PRAY: Lord Jesus, thank You for ruling everything for the good of Your Church. Give us courage and boldness to tell everyone Your great story. Amen.

107

Ten days after Jesus went up into heaven, He sends the Holy Spirit. The Church starts to grow.

Pentecost

What languages do you know? Which would you like to learn?

After Jesus ascended into heaven, His disciples went back into Jerusalem. When they were gathered together, Peter told them someone needed to take Judas's place as one of the twelve apostles. They considered two men who had been with Jesus from His Baptism until His ascension. After they prayed, Matthias was chosen as the new disciple.

Ten days after Jesus ascended into heaven, there was an old Jewish festival in Jerusalem called Pentecost (PEN-tih-kawst). God had first told Moses about the Festival of Pentecost when they met together on Mount Sinai. Pentecost celebrated the first harvest of the year, when food was gathered and brought in from the fields. Jews came to Jerusalem from all over the world for Pentecost, thus there were many different languages spoken.

On this Pentecost Sunday, Jesus' disciples were gathered together in one place. Suddenly, a loud sound like a fast-blowing wind came from heaven and filled the house where they were. The disciples saw what looked like tongues of fire spread out and rest on everyone. All the people there began speaking in a language they had never studied or learned before. The Holy Spirit gave them power to understand and speak different languages!

Many of the Jews who were gathered in Jerusalem for Pentecost heard the sound and rushed over to see what was going on. Suddenly, they heard the disciples speaking the Good News about Jesus in their own languages they had spoken since they were children.

But some of the Jews who lived in Jerusalem made fun of the disciples and said they were drunk.

When Peter heard this, he got everyone's attention and raised his voice to speak to them. He explained that the disciples were not drunk, but that God had poured out the Holy Spirit, who gave them the ability to speak in the different languages of the Jews gathered together in Jerusalem.

Peter told them this was exactly what the Old Testament prophet Joel had said would happen in the last days when God poured out His Spirit. Then, Peter explained why it had happened: because God had sent Jesus Christ, His Son, the promised Savior to them. Instead of believing in Him, however, they had rejected Him and killed Him on the cross, but God had raised Him from the dead. The disciples had seen Jesus many times after He had risen from the dead, and now they were urging every Jew who heard them to be baptized. That day, three thousand Jews became disciples of Jesus and members of the Church.

Today, the Bible has been written down in many different languages so people all around the world can know how Jesus came to save them. The Holy Spirit came to us at our Baptism to give us faith in Jesus and to keep that faith strong. He gives us courage to tell other people about Jesus and works to give them faith when they hear.

Jesus gives Peter and John power to heal a man who can't walk. He runs, leaps, and praises God.

Peter and John Heal a Man Who Can't Walk

What would you say to someone who doesn't care about Jesus?

One day, Peter and John passed a beggar on their way to the temple. This man's legs were so weak he had never in his whole life been able to walk. At that time, if you couldn't walk, then you couldn't work, so the man begged for money, hoping the people who passed by would feel sorry for him and give him some.

When he saw Peter and John, he asked them for some money. Peter told him, "Look at us." The man looked closely at them, expecting some money. Peter told him, "I have no silver and gold, but what I do have I give to you. In the name of Jesus Christ of Nazareth, rise up and walk!" Peter grabbed his right hand and helped him to his feet.

Immediately, the man felt his feet and ankles grow strong, and he leaped up and began walking around. He followed Peter and John into the temple. The people in the temple recognized the beggar and were amazed to see him jumping and leaping. They rushed in to take a closer look.

Peter asked them, "Men of Israel, why do you wonder at this?" He told them the God of their fathers Abraham, Isaac, and Jacob had given Jesus glory, but they had handed Him over to Pilate to be killed. They had denied Jesus, the promised Messiah, and had asked Pilate to release the murderer Barabbas instead of Jesus. They had killed the Son of God, who had created all life. But God had raised Jesus from the dead, and Peter and John and all the apostles were witnesses who had seen Him alive. Peter told them Jesus had healed the beggar and made him strong.

Peter told the people they had not known what they were doing when they had crucified Jesus, but now was the time to be sorry for what they had done and ask God to forgive them for Jesus' sake.

The Jewish priests did not like what Peter and John were saying, and they sent guards to arrest them and put them in jail for the night. The next morning, the Jewish leaders met, but they couldn't do anything because everyone in Jerusalem knew the man, and it was clear that he had been healed. So all they could do was warn Peter and John to stop talking about Jesus.

Peter told the priests they had to decide for themselves what was right and wrong. But Peter, John, and Jesus' other apostles had to do what God sent them to do.

Some people don't like us to talk about Jesus. But Jesus commanded us to tell everyone He loves them and wants to save them. We won't be rude and pushy; we won't make them talk about God if they don't want to. But we will pray for Jesus to show us the right time to talk and ask Him to help us speak boldly when that time comes.

LET'S PRAY: Holy Father, thank You for giving Peter and John healing power so the people at the temple were ready to listen closely to what Peter told them. Give me courage to speak, and make other people ready to listen to the Good News about Jesus, their Savior. Amen.

A follower named Stephen boldly tells the Jewish leaders about Jesus, and they have him killed.

Stephen, the First Christian to Die

Acts 6–7

Why is it so hard to be nice to someone who has hurt you?

As the twelve apostles taught about Jesus in the temple, many Jews believed and were baptized. The Early Church started to grow very quickly. Among the Christians, there were many widows, women whose husbands had died and didn't have money to take care of themselves. The Christians took up offerings to buy food for them.

The problem was that the widows from Jerusalem were getting taken care of, but not the widows from far away. When the apostles learned about it, they were concerned. They wanted to make sure everyone who needed help got taken care of, but Jesus had sent them to preach the Good News, not to serve tables. They said, "Brothers, pick out seven men who are full of the Spirit and of wisdom, whom we will appoint to this duty." These men would make sure every person got help. One of those seven men was named Stephen.

Stephen was full of grace and power by the Holy Spirit. He did great miracles, just like the apostles were doing. When some Jews who didn't believe in Jesus started arguing with him, the Holy Spirit made Stephen so wise he proved they were wrong. Sadly, they didn't believe Stephen. They just got more angry with him.

They took Stephen to the high priest, Caiaphas, and also to the same Jewish court that had decided to put Jesus to death. The Jewish court looked at Stephen and noticed his face was like an angel's face, probably glowing.

The Holy Spirit made Stephen very, very wise. Stephen told the Jewish leaders about all the times in the Old Testament when God had raised up a leader for His people Israel but the Israelites had refused to follow him. He talked about leaders like Joseph, Moses, and King David—and how the Israelites had grumbled against them and refused to obey them. And now, when God had sent His own promised Son, they had done even worse to Him—they had betrayed and murdered Jesus.

When the priests and other leaders heard this, they got so mad they put their fingers in their ears, rushed together at Stephen, dragged him outside, and picked up big stones and rocks to throw at him and kill him.

As Stephen was being stoned, he prayed to Jesus, "Lord Jesus, receive my spirit." He said, "Lord, do not hold this sin against them." Then Stephen died, and his spirit went to heaven.

One of the hardest things for us to do is to forgive people who are hurting us—especially if they do it because we believe in Jesus. But the Holy Spirit made Stephen strong, and He can make you strong to pray for those who hurt you and to boldly tell everyone the Good News of what Jesus did to save us all.

LET'S PRAY: Lord Jesus, thank You for giving the Holy Spirit to make Stephen so bold and strong. Give me Your Holy Spirit too, so I can have the courage to tell others about You, especially when people want to hurt me for believing in You. Amen.

Saul wants to destroy Jesus' followers. After Jesus appears to him on a road, Saul believes in Him.

What would you do if someone who had always been really mean to you suddenly wanted to be your friend?

Earlier in Acts, a Christian named Stephen, who told the Good News about Jesus, was killed by the Jewish leaders, who threw big stones and rocks at him. As they got ready to throw the stones, the Jewish leaders took off their coats and laid them at the feet of a young man named Saul, who also thought Stephen should die for believing in Jesus.

Saul believed Jesus was a false teacher who taught lies about God and pretended to be God's Son. He wanted to stop the Christians from telling other people about Jesus, so he went from house to house through Jerusalem, dragging off the people who believed in Jesus and putting them in prison.

Saul wanted to attack the Christians in Damascus, so the high priest wrote letters for him so that if he found any believers in Jesus, he could tie them up and bring them back to Jerusalem.

When Saul came near Damascus, "suddenly a light from heaven shone around him." He fell to the ground and heard a voice calling, "Saul, Saul, why are you persecuting Me?" Saul asked, "Who are You, Lord?" The voice answered, "I am Jesus, whom you are persecuting. But rise and enter the city, and you will be told what you are to do."

The men traveling with Saul heard the voice, but they didn't see anyone. Saul got up off the ground, but when he opened his eyes he couldn't see anything. The men took his hand and led him into Damascus. For three days, Saul was unable to see. He didn't eat or drink anything during this time.

Then, Jesus told a Christian in Damascus named Ananias (an-uh-NIGH-uhs) to go and lay his hands on Saul so he could see again. Ananias was scared of Saul, but he obeyed Jesus. He went and laid his hands on Saul, and Jesus gave Saul back his sight. Ananias baptized him.

Right there in Damascus, Saul began teaching that Jesus was the Christ, the Savior of the world. Some Jews got angry and made plans to kill Saul. But Saul found out and had his disciples lower him down in a basket through an opening in the wall.

Saul returned to Jerusalem, but the Christians there were afraid of him. A devout Christian named Barnabas took Saul to the apostles and described how Jesus had appeared to Saul on the road to Damascus. The apostles welcomed Saul, and he became known as Paul.

Sometimes, people do very bad things that hurt us. Even if they start being nice, we don't know if we can trust them or not. But Jesus loves them just like He loves us. And He can change them so they can work hard for their Savior and for all of us Christians.

LET'S PRAY: Lord Jesus, thank You for loving Saul, even though he did horrible things to Your people. Remind me that You suffered and died for all people—even those who treat me very badly. Help me to forgive them and pray for them, that they may believe You are their Savior too. Amen.

Peter is in jail for teaching about Jesus. But during the night, an angel comes and sets him free.

Peter Is Freed from Prison

When bad and scary things happen to you, where do you think God is?

While Paul began sharing his new faith, Peter and the other apostles continued to boldly tell people the Good News about Jesus. That's when a new King Herod decided to attack the Church. His grandfather was King Herod the Great, the king who tried to kill little Jesus after the Wise Men came. His uncle was Herod Antipas, who killed John the Baptist.

Like the other Herods, this one wanted the Jewish rulers to like him, so he arrested John's brother James and had him killed. That made James the first of the twelve apostles to die for Jesus. When Herod learned he had made the Jewish leaders happy by killing James, he arrested Peter and announced he would bring him out and kill him after the Passover. Many Christians heard the terrible news, gathered together, and spent the night praying for Jesus to save Peter.

Late that night, Peter was in jail sleeping between two guards, who were both chained to him. Suddenly, in the middle of the night, an angel appeared in Peter's cell, and a light shone around him. The angel struck Peter on the side and said, "Get up quickly." When he got up, the chains fell off his hands. The angel told Peter to get dressed and follow him. At first, Peter didn't think this was actually happening; he thought Jesus was giving him a vision.

The angel led him past the first guard and the second. When they came near the iron gate that led into the city, it opened by itself. The angel led him along one street and then immediately left him. That's when Peter realized Jesus had really set him free.

He went to the house where the Christians were praying for him, and he knocked on the door. A servant girl named Rhoda recognized his voice. She was so excited that she left him outside while she ran in to tell the others that Peter was there. At first they told her, "You are out of your mind." But then they heard Peter knocking at the door. They opened it, saw Peter, and were amazed. He waved his hand to quiet them down; then, he told them how God had saved him. He said, "Tell these things to James and to the brothers." This James was the brother of Jesus, the leader of the Church in Jerusalem. Then, Peter left to go to another city where he could safely teach people about Jesus.

God always watches over us—even when bad things happen to us. Though King Herod killed James, Jesus had promised James that He would raise him from the grave at the Last Day. He set Peter free so he could keep telling the Good News about Jesus. You can trust God to watch over you and never let anything keep you out of His home in heaven.

LET'S PRAY: Lord Jesus, thank You for taking James home to heaven and protecting Peter so he could stay and tell Your story to people who needed to hear it. Give me faith to trust You and courage to share the Good News of Your love wherever I am. Amen.

Once Saul tried to destroy Christians. Now, also known as Paul, he travels around teaching people about Jesus.

Paul's First Missionary Journey

Describe a time you were asked to do something important.

While Peter went from place to place sharing the Good News about Jesus, Paul and Barnabas were living in a town called Antioch. They met some very fine and strong Christians there. One time while the people in the Antioch church were praying, the Holy Spirit told them, "Set apart for Me Barnabas and Saul [Paul] for the work to which I have called them." The Christians prayed and laid their hands on the heads of Barnabas and Paul. Then, the Holy Spirit sent them off to go and visit new places and tell the people there about Jesus' life, death, and resurrection.

You might remember that when the Holy Spirit came at Pentecost, Jerusalem was filled with Jews who had gathered in town from all over the world for the feast. Instead of keeping His Church in Jerusalem, God was now sending believers out into the world with the Good News of Jesus. They left the land of Israel, and the Church grew bigger and began to spread out into the world.

Every time Paul and Barnabas entered a new city, they looked for Jews and their synagogues. That's because Jews were spread out all over the Roman Empire. Barnabas and Paul could find a synagogue in most of the towns they went to. That is where they started. They went to the synagogue on the Sabbath Day, Saturday, and taught the Jews there about Jesus. Then, on the other days of the week, they talked about Jesus to everyone they met, Jews and Gentiles.

They were doing the same thing Jesus had done when He went preaching throughout the land of Israel. Whenever He entered a town or village, He went to the services at the synagogues on the Sabbath and taught them about God's kingdom. Then, during the week, He visited and talked with people wherever He met them: on the streets, at wells, in the marketplaces, or in people's houses.

As Barnabas and Paul shared the faith in the towns where they traveled, the Jews and Gentiles who believed in Jesus gathered together and started to form churches. God was with them, and in the cities where they traveled, many people came to believe. Barnabas and Paul picked leaders who were strong believers, taught them to be pastors, and put them in charge of the congregations while they moved on to the next town.

God may not call you to be a missionary, leave your country, and go to live in distant places teaching people about Jesus, but He might. He may not call you to be a pastor or a teacher in some other part of our country, but He might. But even if God doesn't call you to be a missionary, pastor, or teacher, He does send you to your classmates, friends, neighbors, and even people you don't know so you can tell them about Jesus and how He loves them and died for them. The Holy Spirit will guide you and teach you exactly what to say.

LET'S PRAY: Lord Jesus, thank You for making Barnabas and Paul's missionary journeys so successful. Help me tell my friends and others about You so they might also believe and learn how great You are. Amen.

119

God breaks Paul and Silas's chains. They tell the jailer about Jesus and baptize him and his family.

Paul and Silas in Prison

Acts 16:16–40

Have you ever gotten in trouble for doing something nice?

Paul finished his first missionary journey with Barnabas; then, he told his friend they should go back and see how the new churches were doing. Barnabas liked the idea and wanted to take along his cousin Mark (who later wrote the Gospel of Mark). But Paul didn't think that was a good idea.

Mark had gone with them on their first missionary journey, but right in the middle he had left to go back home, even though Barnabas and Paul still needed him. Paul didn't want that to happen again. Barnabas said it wouldn't, but Paul didn't want to take the chance. Since they couldn't agree, they split up to go to different places. Paul brought along his friend Silas, while Barnabas took Mark along with him to a different place.

Paul and Silas came to a city called Philippi (fih-LIPP-eye). They talked to a group of people, and the Holy Spirit created faith in a wealthy woman named Lydia. She welcomed them to stay in her house.

As Paul and Silas shared the Gospel in the city, a slave girl who had a demon followed them around, saying, "These men are servants of the Most High God, who proclaim to you the way of salvation." Paul turned and said to the demon, "I command you in the name of Jesus Christ to come out of her." And the demon immediately left her.

That made the people mad who owned the slave girl. Back when she still had the demon, they had earned a lot of money from others who wanted her to tell their futures. But now with the demon gone, their chance to make a lot of money was gone. They grabbed Paul and Silas and dragged them before the judges.

The judges ordered that they be beaten with rods and put in prison for the night. But Paul and Silas didn't sit around feeling sorry for themselves. Around midnight, they were praying and singing in their prison cell, and all the other prisoners were listening. Suddenly, a strong earthquake struck, and all the prison doors opened up and the chains fell off of every prisoner.

The jailer who was in charge of the prison woke up and got really scared. He saw the jail doors standing open and thought all the prisoners had escaped. Since he thought that he had failed to keep them in jail, he pulled out his sword to kill himself. But Paul shouted that he should not hurt himself, because all the prisoners were still there. The jailer asked for a torch and ran inside to see. He fell down in front of Paul and Silas and asked what he had to do to be saved. Paul told him, "Believe in the Lord Jesus, and you will be saved, you and your household." Then, Paul and Silas told the jailer and his family and servants all about Jesus. They baptized his whole household.

Sometimes, we try to be nice to people but they treat us very badly. That may make you want to stop being nice and telling people about Jesus. But remember Paul and Silas. Pray to Jesus and sing hymns to say thanks to Him. He will take away your sorrow and fill you with His joy. The Holy Spirit will show you how you can teach someone about Jesus.

LET'S PRAY: Lord Jesus, thank You for the bold faith of Paul and Silas. Give me such thankfulness and courage that people will want to know all about You. Amen.

Paul is traveling in a ship when a great storm wrecks it. God brings everyone safely to shore.

Name someplace you wanted to go or something you wanted to do but couldn't.

After Paul and Silas were freed from prison and finished the second missionary journey, they rested a bit. Then, they took a third journey that ended in Jerusalem. On this journey, they preached the Gospel and performed miracles in Jesus' name, such as when Jesus raised a young man named Eutychus (YOO-tih-kuhs) from the dead through Paul (see Acts 20:7–12). In each city, they found Jews and Gentiles who were glad to hear the Good News about Jesus, but there were also many who tried to make them stop.

While Paul was at the temple in Jerusalem, he was spotted by some of the Jews who had tried to stop him during his missionary journeys. They cried for help, telling the Jews of Jerusalem that Paul was bringing Gentiles into the temple against God's Law. They grabbed Paul and started beating him—even though no Gentiles were in the temple with him.

Then, soldiers from the Roman army marched in, grabbed Paul, and took him to safety. Since some Jews made plans to attack and kill him in Jerusalem, the Roman soldiers took him out of town at night on horseback and led him to a safe place called Caesarea (sez-uh-REE-uh).

Paul had wanted to go on and travel to new parts of the Roman Empire to share the Good News about Jesus, but he had to stay under guard in Caesarea for two years until the new governor, Festus, came. Festus planned to take Paul to Jerusalem for his trial, but Paul knew the Jews there were planning to kill him. So he asked to have his trial before the Roman Emperor, and Paul was put on a ship to sail across the sea to Rome.

Along the way, a strong storm came up that lasted for two whole weeks! Finally, on the fourteenth day, they saw an island beach and tried to sail the ship there, but it struck ground and the powerful waves tore it into pieces. Everyone jumped into the water and made it safely to shore.

But they were all wet, and the night was cold and rainy. The island people started a big fire to warm the travelers. As Paul was gathering sticks, a snake came out and bit him on the hand. The island people thought God was punishing Paul and watched for him to die from the snakebite. But Paul's hand did not swell up, and he didn't fall over and die. So the people thought he must be a god instead. The chief man on the island welcomed Paul to his house, and Paul healed the man's father, who was sick with a fever. After that, sick people from the island came, and Jesus healed all of them through Paul. The journey and shipwreck gave Paul the chance to share the story of Jesus with the soldiers, the sailors, and now the people from the island.

Like Paul, we sometimes find that life doesn't go the way we want it to, and we go through hard times. But Jesus promises He will always be with us, no matter what happens. He will even use the hard times in our lives to reach other people with the Good News, and He will guide us safely to live with Him in heaven.

LET'S PRAY: Lord Jesus, You watched carefully over Paul and everyone with him on that boat. Help me know You will always be with me so I will never need to be afraid. Amen.

Jesus' disciple John is forced to live on an island.
Jesus promises He will come back on the Last Day.

What things make you bold and strong when you get discouraged?

Peter and Paul spent their last days in Rome, and some say that both were put to death on the same day. All but one of Jesus' twelve apostles were put to death for their faith in Jesus. The last of the Twelve was John, the brother of James, who took care of Mary after Jesus died.

John wasn't put to death, but he was exiled. He was forced to leave his people and live on an island called Patmos (PAT-mahs). For an apostle, being away from Christians was one of the hardest things.

But something very important happened while John was in exile. Jesus showed him a revelation that God the Father had given Him. It showed John what was happening in heaven and on earth.

That is so important because sometimes really bad things happen. Sometimes, it feels like Jesus doesn't know what's happening to us or He doesn't care about us. Jesus gave John this revelation to write down so we could remember that God is in control of everything that happens in this world, and one day He will come again to take away all the bad things and make His creation new, perfect, and wonderful forever—and that includes each of us believers too.

In the revelation, John saw Jesus in heaven. He wrote about it: "I saw . . . one like a son of man. . . . The hairs of His head were white, like white wool, like snow. His eyes were like a flame of fire, His feet were like burnished bronze, refined in a furnace, and His voice was like the roar of many waters. . . . His face was like the sun shining in full strength" (Revelation 1:12–16).

John was very scared when he saw the glory of Jesus, the Son of God. He fell at our Savior's feet like he was dead. But Jesus laid His hand on John and told him not to be afraid: "Fear not, I am the first and the last, and the living one. I died, and behold I am alive forevermore. . . . Write therefore the things that you have seen, those that are and those that are to take place after this" (Revelation 1:17–19).

So John wrote it all down in what became the last book of the Bible, Revelation. It tells us that God supervises all things and orders events so unbelievers will repent and glorify Him.

John finished his Book of Revelation with a promise from Jesus: "Surely I am coming soon." John's answer is our prayer, "Amen. Come, Lord Jesus!" (Revelation 22:20).

During this life, you will have good times and bad, happy times and sad. But Jesus will never leave you. He will guard and protect you, and on the Last Day He will come back to punish Satan and all his demons. But for us who love Jesus and look forward to His return, He will make us shine like the stars in heaven and give us a new heaven and a new earth.

LET'S PRAY: Lord Jesus, thank You for coming the first time at Bethlehem to save us, for coming today to teach us with Your words, and for Your promise to come on the Last Day to make this earth new and perfect forever. Keep me in this faith until You return. Amen.